*Foreword by Sister Maria del Rey
of Maryknoll*

NUN

A Gallery of Sisters

by Kathleen Elgin

Random House, New York

NIHIL OBSTAT

Gall Higgins, O.F.M.Cap.
CENSOR LIBRORUM

IMPRIMATUR

✠ *Francis Cardinal Spellman*
ARCHBISHOP OF NEW YORK

The *nihil obstat* and *imprimatur* are official declaration that a book or pamphlet is free of doctrinal or moral error. No implication is contained therein that those who have granted the *nihil obstat* and *imprimatur* agree with the contents, opinions or statements expressed.

June 4, 1964

Table of Contents

Each Sister depicted in these stories was chosen by Sisters in the orders of today to represent their communities as an "outstanding Sister." The choices were theirs alone.

Kathleen Elgin

To F. L.

Foreword

BEING A SISTER is rather like the circus feat of riding two horses at once. The trick is to keep one's feet planted firmly on each animal, but at the same time allow for slips and starts and individual differences.

Sometimes a Sister seems to put her weight entirely on the Religious Life; sometimes on what, for lack of a better term, we call the World. At times she is all absorbed in prayer, silence, thoughts of God, quiet love for Him and for all men. At others, she is efficiency plus—looking over blueprints for a new hospital, checking sources for a doctoral thesis, questioning a salesman who may have school desks, thumbtacks or a revolutionary potato-peeler to sell. But no matter what the urgency of the moment, there is always that other life galloping alongside.

Miss Elgin's book captures the spirit of both lives—that nice balance which enables a Sister to give everything to God and, at the same time, throw herself whole-heartedly into good works for men. One sees here that the often quaint garments clothe a real woman, one who has no children that she may love all children more.

Not many girls are called to live two lives at once. She who attempts it must have a good sense of rhythm and adequate training. More than that, she must love both lives and understand them perfectly. But I can attest that once she has control over them and has them pointed in the right direction, straight to God's heart so full of love for men, she is in for an exhilarating ride.

—Sister Maria del Rey of Maryknoll

Over the centuries, thousands of young women have felt the call to enter Sisterhoods . . . to become nuns. They have endured poverty, starvation, torture, and have given their lives to unselfish teaching, nursing, caring for and protecting all kinds of people of all ages.

hy?

"Whys?" surround the young girl who enters the Sisterhood.

"Why?" is often spoken by her parents, or by her classmates, who have spent the growing-up years with her; or perhaps by the young man who thought of one day becoming her husband.

"Why?" is the word spoken by her mother, who thinks of the grandchildren she would have looked out for later on; by the father who, seeing a definite talent in his daughter, had planned her education with pride.

"Why?" is the word spoken by the young girl herself, and often the answer is . . .

"I was
chosen,
I did not
choose . . .
it is something
I cannot
explain,
something
you cannot
understand . . ."

The answers
to "Why?" are
also these:

"St. Ursula's life
has influenced me to be-
come a teacher."

"The works of
Dr. Albert Schweitzer
impressed me greatly, and
I felt that I could best serve
God and the people of
Africa by using my skills
as a doctor in a
Sisterhood."

"I saw the movie
The Keys of the Kingdom.
Then I read an article
about a tribe of unciv-
ilized Indians in South
America. I want to take
the word of God and the
knowledge of science
to them . . ."

"I joined the

Dominicans so that I could
give my life to teaching and
helping the very young of
our country . . ."

Today most Sisterhoods use psychological and vocational testing to determine the motivations and abilities of the young hopefuls. This realistically and dramatically demands of each girl "Why?"

As the psychological test has moved into the convents, nuns have moved out into the world. As we on the outside see them more and more, our curiosity grows . . . The silent gliding figure in the rustling black habit . . . is this a real person . . . are nuns . . . *people*?

This smiling Columban sister plays the cello in a small orchestra, plays a recorder, makes tapes and sometimes broadcasts on radio or TV. Sister Mary Barbara *is* a very real person . . . with a difference . . . she knows of the world, but even more,

16

realizes the unseen power behind it.

Yes, nuns *are* people, dedicated, obedient, giving—through their
devotion, they are able to help and
teach, to enlighten, in hospitals, in
schools, in missions here and abroad.

List of Sisterhoods and Dates of Founding

1206 DOMINICAN SISTERS OF ADRIAN, O.P.

1212 POOR CLARE NUNS, O.S.C.

1233 SERVANTS OF MARY, O.S.M.

1562 DISCALCED CARMELITE NUNS, O.C.D.

1597 SCHOOL SISTERS OF NOTRE DAME, S.S.N.D.

1606 SISTERS OF THE COMPANY OF MARY, O.D.N.

1610 VISITATION NUNS, V.H.M.

1633 DAUGHTERS OF CHARITY OF ST. VINCENT de PAUL, D.C.

1636 RELIGIOUS HOSPITALERS OF ST. JOSEPH, R.H.S.J.

1639 SACRAMENTINE NUNS, R.S.

1641 SISTERS OF THE GOOD SHEPHERD, R.G.S.

1648 SISTERS OF ST. JOSEPH OF CORONDOLET, C.S.J.

1703 DAUGHTERS OF WISDOM, D.W.

1706 DAUGHTERS OF THE HOLY GHOST, F.S.E.

1738 THE GREY NUNS OF THE SACRED HEART, G.N.S.H.

1803 SISTERS OF NOTRE DAME de NAMUR, S.N.D.

1812 SISTERS OF CHARITY OF NAZARETH, S.C.N.

1825 SISTERS OF OUR LADY OF MT. CARMEL, O. CARM.

1829 OBLATE SISTERS OF PROVIDENCE, O.S.P.

1833 SISTERS OF CHARITY OF THE BLESSED VIRGIN MARY, B.V.M.

1835 SISTERS OF CHARITY, S.C.

1840 SISTERS OF PROVIDENCE, S.P

1842 SISTERS OF THE HOLY FAMILY, S.S.F.

1843 SISTERS OF MERCY OF THE UNION IN THE U.S.A., R.S.M.

1843 SISTERS OF THE HOLY CROSS, C.S.C.

1845 MARIST MISSIONARY SISTERS, S.M.S.M.

1849 SISTERS OF THE THIRD ORDER OF ST. FRANCIS OF ASSISI, O.S.F.

1851 SISTERS, SERVANTS OF MARY, S. de M.

1867 MISSIONARY SISTERS OF VERONA, M.S.V.

1869 MISSIONARY SISTERS OF OUR LADY OF AFRICA, WHITE SISTERS, W.S.

1897 MISSIONARY SISTERS OF THE IMMACULATE HEART OF MARY, I.C.M.

1900 SERVANTS OF RELIEF FOR INCURABLE CANCER, O.P.

1910 MISSIONARY SISTERS OF THE IMMACULATE CONCEPTION OF THE MOTHER OF GOD, S.M.I.C.

1912 MARYKNOLL SISTERS, O.P.

1915 DAUGHTERS OF ST. PAUL, D.S.P.

1922 MISSIONARY SISTERS OF ST. COLUMBAN, S.S.C.

1922 MISSIONARY SISTERS OF OUR LADY OF THE ANGELS, M.N.D.A.

1925 MEDICAL MISSION SISTERS, S.C.M.M.

18

Decision

THE FIRST NUN COULD HAVE BEEN A GIRL with a natural talent for nursing . . . she could have been a born teacher . . . she could have been St. Macrina, sister of St. Basil, founder of probably the oldest order of nuns, in 358 A.D.

No matter who it was, she became a nun because her love for God was greater than for things of the world. The root source of a vocation to the service of God is love. And she was one of the women who joined with the early monks in their humane work with the sick, poor and persecuted. Groups of these women who volunteered their help were formed into various communities, or orders, of nuns, in co-ordination and co-operation with the monks.

Through the centuries, from 358 A.D., there followed the Benedictines . . . the Dominicans . . . the Carmelites . . . and the Ursulines. As these orders were established, laws were made to govern and control them, and gradually the Church set universal standards and requirements for those entering the convent; requirements of character, health, mental stability and age.

For instance, a girl can apply for admission to an order, but as Canon law says, she cannot be accepted before she is sixteen; just as she cannot marry before sixteen without a court order nor before eighteen without parents' consent. (Most orders do not take anyone over thirty-five.)

If a girl decides to become a nun in a surge of pious feeling and emotion —a "Joan of Arc" complex—her decision is not a true one. Cobwebby mysticism is not wanted at all. Self-analysis and common sense must be in the foreground. There must be the desire to give, not take; a desire to live life in obedient service, to give the utmost of skill, talent and knowledge, every day, every hour, in complete dedication.

There is no mystery in a religious vocation. It is wanting to live with God, to live with the love of God; it is simply a matter of love. Then how best to express this love—which religious order is *the* one for any particular girl?

There are about two hundred and fifty different religious orders in the

United States, doing all kinds of service. Some care for the aged, some staff orphanages. Others do hospital work. One does only medical work; these Sisters are technicians, anesthetists, nurses, doctors and surgeons. By Papal decree in 1936 Sisters were permitted to study medicine and surgery.

Many, many orders are devoted to teaching; the parochial school system is the backbone of the Catholic Church in America. No finer career exists than that of teaching the young, of helping to form the next generation. Then, too, there is social service work, and domestic work in the seminaries.

A vast field is mission work in this country and in many foreign lands; the work is arduous, often dangerous, but the rewards are great. For centuries mission Sisters have followed the trail-breaking efforts of the priests on every continent.

In addition to these so-called "active orders," there are the "contemplative," the cloistered Sisters. Their life is one devoted to prayer and adoration, the making of altar cloths and vestments, the bread for the Holy Eucharist.

Many kind-hearted women nurse and teach, care for the poor and work in seminaries; many wives and mothers can be called "dedicated" in the truest sense of the word. The hardships and the rewards of mission life are no greater for Sisters than for lay workers. But if in addition to the desire to serve man there is the deep urge to live with God, to choose Him for the deepest core of her life, to make every minute and every task swing around Him as a mother's does for her family, then she is ready for and has chosen religious life.

Each order has its own individuality and each girl must find her own particular niche in the scheme of things. When she finds the *right* order for her choice of career, it is then that she makes the final decision to become a nun. She is ready to serve man and love God. The common denominator of all orders is a chance to live life for God, doing His Will.

Then the seemingly endless routine of papers begins: application papers, character recommendations, physical and mental health certificates, baptism papers, birth certificates and educational credits. The Sisterhood then studies the application, carefully and thoroughly, screens the details and weighs the personality of the girl against the standards and purpose of the order. Canon law says that both the candidate and the congregation must make the decision freely. No one can be forced to come, and nobody can force the religious order to accept anyone.

After acceptance, she must take with her to the convent certain specified things—among them, black nylon stockings, black or gray sweaters, and the ultra-sensible shoes which have come to characterize the nun. With these also she must bring her dowry, an amount of money which varies with each order. This dowry is invested for her, and if ever there is a reason for her to leave the convent, the money is returned—a sort of basic security. Sometimes an order will accept as a dowry a special education, talent or skill.

The decision has been made . . . everything is ready . . . the next step is the one leading to the convent door.

Sister Miriam Michael, O.P.

IT WAS DURING HER THREE YEARS of graduate science study that Sister Miriam Michael first learned that man is not isolated from his fellow man either by reason of religious profession or by reason of the laboratory.

She studied in the seclusion of the laboratory and the library, but she did not live in the seclusion of a parish house. Her convent was located in a slum district, and she learned first-hand what is meant by overcrowded housing, lack of recreational facilities, and sickness due to poor sanitation and undernourishment.

After receiving her master of science degree, Sister Michael went to teach at Siena Heights College in Adrian, Michigan. Here she enjoyed the

freedom of combining the stimulation of teaching and the quiet reward of research in the biochemistry laboratory.

The uncertainty with which she began her teaching developed into confidence. But each avenue that she turned up in research was closed, not only because of lack of equipment, but her own limitations in educational background.

So for eight years, until 1948, she became a summer student at Michigan State, Illinois Tech and Michigan University, in whichever institution would benefit most directly her research in infrared spectroscopy. Interest in and grants for science research were not what they are today, and the Spectroscopy Laboratory at Illinois Institute of Technology was housed in the basement of an 1880-vintage building standing between the Rock Island Railroad tracks and Lake Michigan.

Yet it was there, with an instrument made in the local shop, using galvanometer tracings made in spite of the vibrations of too-frequent trains, that Sister Michael learned the rudiments of infrared spectroscopy. There, too, as in every laboratory into which she went in the United States or Europe, she found that religion and science can work side by side.

She gave something significant by making the scientists aware of the contributing role of a Sister in the laboratory. They enriched her by their friendly acceptance and banter and made her more firm in her conviction that infrared spectroscopy had given her the tool to investigate the molecular structure of nucleic acid derivatives.

The return to her small research laboratory at Siena Heights brought the sharp realization of the lack of financial resources for equipment. However, the Research Corporation gave an initial grant which helped to purchase an infrared spectrophotometer, but without accessories. It was like buying a car without the chassis or lights, and settling for the essential frame, wheels, motor and brakes. However, with the stripped-down instrument she began some work in infrared, began the first fumbling attempts to record the spectra of nucleic acid derivatives.

Next she needed an extrusion press, and was able to use one in a tool and die shop of a local factory, during the men's lunch hour. Under the critical eye of an old craftsman, Sister Michael approached the final solution of the problem in the development of of the now almost universally employed potassium bromide (Kbr) disk technique. The intrigued and helpful shopmen were kind to this nun who hurried in and out of the shop on off-union hours.

24

An invitation to speak before a local technical club indirectly answered her need for a power press. After her talk, there followed an excited two-hour discussion, and one of the men in her audience called Sister the next day asking if she would have the time to look at a press that was presently not in use. Sister Michael would have gone almost anywhere at any time for a press! So it was that she converted a large electrically operated extrusion press to meet her needs; senior chemistry majors were able to help in the weighing of mixtures and in pressing them into what eventually became glasslike disks of Kbr and the desired chemical.

Sister Michael presented the method of sample preparation and its advantages before the Ohio State University Symposium on Molecular Structure in 1951. Within two weeks requests began pouring in from laboratories all around the country, as well as from Europe, for more details and reprints of her talk. So she gave to scientific colleagues in many biochemical laboratories a tool they could broadly and thoroughly exploit—a technique for analyzing solids by means of infrared absorption.

Then came the formal invitation to deliver the endowed Peter C. Reilly Lectures in Chemistry, at Notre Dame in 1953, the first woman so honored. After that, invitations to the Sorbonne for an international meeting . . . to Heidelberg . . . to Tübingen, where she met Dr. U. Scheidt, who pioneered the Kbr disk technique in Germany . . . to Bristol, where Dr. J. M. McOrmie exploited the paper chromatography technique that she had just missed . . . to Rome for an audience with Pope Pius XII . . . to the cloister of the Holy Cross in Regensburg, Bavaria, from which four Sisters had ventured to the United States more than one hundred years before.

She returned from this stimulating trip to Siena Heights, where her recent years have been spent in the development of a graduate program to provide opportunity for research for secondary teachers. Her sense of accomplishment now is not found in the tributes to her research efforts but in the progress of her students, religious and lay. She has reached the high point of her career, trying to formulate questions and problems in the field of radiation for students in grade school so that they may learn early the provisional nature of science and may thrill to the hidden beauty that the scientist senses in God's world about him.

St. Clare, O.S.C.

THE STORY OF ST. CLARE is inexorably bound up with that of St. Francis of Assisi, for their common destiny was to found the great Order of St. Clares.

In front of the Cathedral of San Giorgio, on the ancient square of Assisi, stood Francis Bernardone. Before Bishop Guido and an incredulous crowd of villagers, he renounced all earthly wealth and possessions. From that time on, dressed in the shabbiest peasant robes, he roamed the green Umbrian plains around Assisi, begging bread, preaching and helping the sick and the poor.

During High Mass on the first Sunday of Lent, Francis had spoken to the thronged cathedral. Clare had been there, in the prayer stall of her noble family, and every ardent, fervent word of the love of Christ spoken by the "Poverello" stayed in her memory. From that day she was to be profoundly and completely influenced by the young friar, founder of the Franciscans. From her cousin Rufino, who had given up his wealth to join Francis in his work, she learned about the life of total renunciation, what it really meant and the joy of spirit and peace of mind it brought.

When he returned to preach the Advent sermons at San Giorgio, Clare was ready to go to Francis and tell him of her decision. She met him secretly, in an olive grove near the small church of Porziuncola, the parish assigned to him by the bishop. These two, the seventeen-year-old girl of an aristocratic family and the dedicated young man of thirty, were of one drive, belief and purpose, and the immediate rapport established between the future Saints lasted their lifetimes.

During that winter of 1211–1212 Clare gradually drifted from the luxurious palace life of her childhood to the life of renunciation. Her family, not comprehending her deep devotion, paid little attention to this "phase," as they called it. But on the night of Palm Sunday, dressed in a pearl-trimmed satin evening robe, she left the noble house of Fevarone Offreduccio through the gate of the dead, opened only to let pass those who were abandoning the house forever.

26

Two brown-clad friars, wearing the cowls of the Umbrian peasant, met Clare outside the walls and, with blazing torches held high, led her to the church of Porziuncola. Francis stood waiting for her, a radiant smile on his face. He led young Clare to the altar and she knelt reverently, her delicate beauty illumined by an inner joy.

Later that Lenten night, in the candlelit nave, Clare stood transformed, as she was to be the rest of her life. The elaborate pearl-studded dress was gone; the shoes of finest Florentine leather were gone. Instead, her slight figure was clad in a rough peasant's tunic, cinched at the waist with a piece of knotted rope. Her feet wore sandals and a veil of white linen draped her shaven head.

And so Francis sent her, as the Abbess Clare, to San Damiano, halfway between Assisi and Porziuncola, a church which Francis had rebuilt from crumbling ruins with his own hands. This little monastery was set in a grove of olive trees at the foot of a gentle slope punctuated by dark scrub growth. A row of cypress trees leaned over a long white stone wall which lined the path leading to the stone sanctuary. Tiny San Damiano—the poor cells in which the Sisters spent the hours, the crude refectory—provided the austere setting for the total sacrifice, the complete poverty and renunciation which Clare and the Poverello accepted.

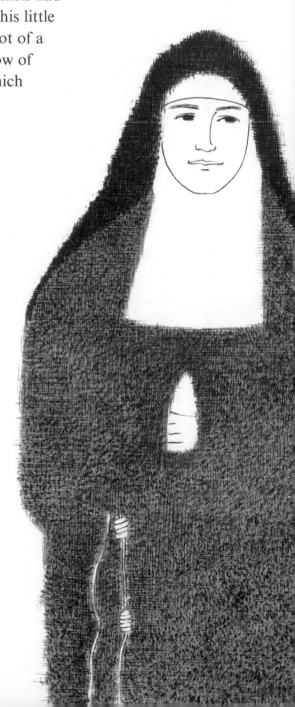

Within these cloistered walls Clare lived the last forty years of her life. One by one they came—Sisters who were to lead a strictly cloistered life of total prayer and penance. In San Damiano, Clare brought to reality the dreams of sacrifice which she and Francis had shared.

Sister Margaret Mary, O.S.M.

AT SEVENTY-FIVE, SISTER MARGARET MARY was keeping up to date on new techniques for teaching Spanish by attending the summer session at Catholic University in Mt. Vernon, Indiana, fifteen hundred miles from her convent.

In this small town, in 1884, Sister Margaret was born Rose Klaus. Six years later she began school, and in a very real sense she has never taken a vacation from learning. On August 15, 1903, she entered the novitiate of the Servants of Mary, founded in this country by the pioneer Sister Mary Gertrude, who had come from the London Motherhouse ten years before.

"On one of the last talks which I had with her before entering the convent," Sister Margaret said, "Mother Gertrude brought up the subject of my delay in entering—my procrastinations, as she put it. After listening patiently to my evasive answers and indecisions, she became rather exhausted. She suddenly leaned toward me, looked steadfastly into my eyes and said kindly but firmly, 'Child, you have not five cents' worth of courage.'

"She got up and walked out of the room, leaving me rather astounded, alone. I, too, rose and flung back this retort: 'Mother, I'll show you how much courage I have.' "

She received the habit of the order in 1904 and the following year made her first profession of vows. Eight years later she was appointed Superior of the convent in Sioux City.

In that year of change for Sister Margaret, there was also a change for the community as a whole. The order was still in the United States in a missionary status; the Sisters were still missionaries. But the country was rapidly outgrowing the position of a mission post! And so the administrative power was broadened, the status was changed to Vicariate.

As the work of the Church in America deepened and extended, the need for even greater independence for all religious communities was a natural corollary. Although there were common roots, the foundations here had developed an essentially American approach and a new freedom had to be established.

Sister Margaret and a companion sister, Sister Mary Emmanuel, with the vision that is part of greatness, initiated the first steps that changed the status of the American community from that of a mission to the present status of a Province.

At eighty Sister Margaret still retained her omnivorous interest in the world of men and affairs that paralleled her consuming interest in the spiritual world to which she had dedicated sixty years of her life, never ceasing to grow and give of her long experience.

Her love of God, her Sisterhood and her country combined to yield a productive life of teaching, inspiring both her students and fellow Sisters.

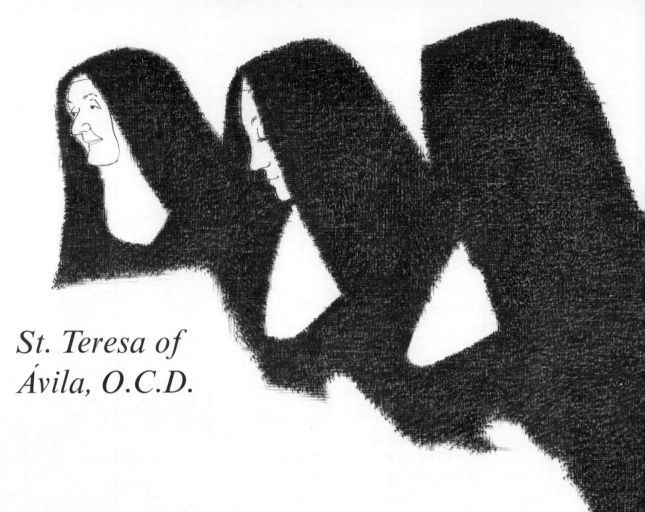

St. Teresa of Ávila, O.C.D.

TERESA DE AHUMADA BECAME SAINT TERESA OF ÁVILA by her superhuman will power and with the grace of God. The evolution of achieving sanctity, her slow and soul-shaking transformation, her visions and ecstasies, made her life unique.

The young Teresa, a spirited product of Spanish nobility, was beautiful, elegant, a coquette overly fond of jewelry and fine clothes; half sinner and half saint, her personality attracted everyone and anyone instantly.

Teresa was painfully aware that she had to fight herself. She fled from the worldly pleasures she loved too much, and in a cold October dawn of 1536, she entered the Convent of the Incarnation in Ávila and a year later pronounced her vows.

In her struggle against self-pride and vanity she often forgot even common sense in controlling harsh penances. Over the years, these excesses ended in attacks of fainting; she endured so much pain, punished her system so continually by rigid fasts that she became a walking skeleton in order to, as she put it, "conquer this body of ours."

These conditions and symptoms became so frequent and severe that one day a rumor began the rounds of the convent:

"Doña Teresa de Ahumada is dying! . . She is dead!"

Teresa was given injections and poultices, she was rubbed with scorpion oil; she was bled and given pills that had to be taken in ones, threes, fives or some other odd number. But the "skill" of the doctors failed, the nuns' prayers were to no avail. Her father took her to a famous "miracle healer" who tried her cures to excess.

Teresa was slowly dying of overtreatment; she asked for the last sacraments. In the next twenty-four hours she gave no sign of life. On the second day hot wax from the candle held by her father fell on her eyelids without causing the slightest reaction.

On the third day, the nuns dug her grave at the convent, and she was washed and wrapped in her shroud. On the fourth day they came to take Teresa for burial, but her father, believed crazy with grief, claimed she was still alive, and would not take his fingers from Teresa's wrist.

The nuns waited. Hours went by. Suddenly Teresa's eyelids showed a brief movement beneath the wax which had sealed the lashes. She was alive, but not returned to life. Acute pain brought her from her trance, but she was able to move just one finger of her right hand. In her delirium she could not lie full length and she lay curled up, her muscles contracted, her knees drawn up to her chin.

After nearly nine months of fever and deep depression she was brought back to the convent, where she spent the next three years in the infirmary, completely paralyzed.

One day she wrote down these awesome words: "When I began to walk on all fours, I thanked God."

She was able to return to her own cell, and dragged herself about the convent. Sheer will gradually returned the use of her legs. Suddenly she could stand erect; she leaned her weight on the soles of her feet, found her balance and walked.

Teresa said that her sins were forgiven her. The nuns around her declared it was a miracle.

She had returned from her long hell to what she now realized was a life of make-believe in the convent. The one hundred and eighty nuns of the Incarnation wore jewelry, chattered and spoke idly during silence times, visited each others' cells and the sound of tambourines and flutes rose above the patio during recreation times. Admirers brought them the latest songs and slipped candies through the grill. They often went to grand homes and castles for dinners or extended visits.

There were a few devout young nuns in the midst of this parody of a cloister, but the ideals of Carmel were difficult to find. The convent was more like a club for single ladies, where each one—according to her rank, wealth and taste—lived in attractive one-room cells or in small apartments. Teresa's cell was detached from the main convent and consisted of two rooms built one above the other. One room looked out upon the garden and here she too received visitors as she sat on floor cushions, working on her embroidery.

Teresa's old conflicts had returned; she was still torn between the world and God. In her apartment one day, Teresa was speaking in her characteristic captivating and persuasive way to a group of young nuns. She described the lives of the holy Fathers of the Desert when the Order of Carmel was first founded. The story of their solitary homage captivated the young women and their feeling was voiced by Teresa's niece, Maria de Ocampo, "Let us go away then, all of us here!"

Her aunt looked up at Maria over her embroidery. To herself she breathed, "Thank God! At last, at last!"

In the agony of her paralysis she had found the real meaning and spirit of God and now she received His command to found a new convent, one devoted to the original idea of Carmel, a cloistered convent with the solitary life, not the hypocritical and superficial life of the Incarnation.

Teresa went to Doña Guiomar de Ulloa, her wealthy friend and benefactor. With no hesitation, she said, "Found your new convent, Teresa. I will help you."

Her first convent was tiny St. Joseph's, just outside of Ávila. At five in the morning of August 24, 1562, the tinkling of a small, cracked bell awoke the people of the San Roque district. The sound guided them to the first chapel ever dedicated to St. Joseph. Mass was said on a spotlessly clean altar, a single extravagance; Teresa gave the habit of coarse frieze to four young girls. Teresa adopted the primitive rule in every single one of its requirements; what was called her reform was actually a return to the original observances of the ancient Order of Carmel. Silence, fasting, bare (or sandaled) feet, and penance; the enclosure door shut on all her Carmelites. For rare visitors the Sister remained invisible behind the barriers of grilles, curtains and veils.

During the five years of enclosure at St. Joseph's, Teresa matured; she became mistress of herself, detached from all egoism or self-interest. At fifty-two, she was still beautiful, gay, lively, more eloquent than ever and endowed with a fantastic charm. It was hard to believe that she was the Teresa who had hovered near death for four days, who had lain paralyzed for years, who had lashed herself with penances, who had doubted herself and her belief. Here was a completely prepossessed woman at the height of her powers. It was then that she began her great foundations.

Dawn of August 13, 1567, disclosed three heavy carts jolting out of Ávila; they contained the essential household articles for the installation of the future convent of Medina del Campo and a few nuns, proud of their leader. Julian de Ávila, the chaplain, followed on horseback. Thus St. Teresa traveled the last fifteen years of her life throughout Spain, in her greatly worn black veil, her frequently darned habit of coarse frieze and her cheap, common rope-soled sandals.

She founded sixteen convents; Teresa had brought the Reform to Carmel.

Sister Mary Alma, S.S.N.D.

SISTER MARY ALMA, PH.D. in biochemistry and physiology, was asked to come to the University of Birmingham, England. Here, in the summer of 1962, along with her American colleague, Dr. Harold Feinberg, she joined the research staff in the biochemistry laboratories of Professor S. B. Perry, one of the top scientists in his field.

This small, alert School Sister was in her element, for this would be her sixth summer session in her kind of research, basic cardiovascular research, which involves working on the hearts of rabbits "in vivo," alive, or "in vitro," in the test tube. The observations made from these careful experiments in metabolism provide more understanding of the mysteries of the human heart, which eventually brings to doctors more knowledge and creates improvements in clinical techniques.

When Sister Mary Alma left the university laboratories at the end of the summer, she returned to the College of Notre Dame of Maryland, to continue research and to teach, as head of the Department of Biological Sciences. Once a winner of the Ehrlich-Krupnik Research Fellowship, she is a nationally acknowledged scholar on the subject of cardiac metabolism and the use of radioisotopes. This enviable reputation has brought many grants to her department: from the National Science Foundation, the National Heart Foundation, the American Medical Association, the Michael Reese Hospital and the Atomic Energy Commission.

These grants have furnished the laboratories at the college with the finest of instruments and equipment, the most complete of any college of its size. But more and more space is needed for this equipment and for more students with their experiments and ideas; more space is needed for future expansion. Sister Mary Alma is working toward the financing of a whole new Science Building, to house laboratories for advanced biochemistry, physiology, research and radiation experiments. She says: "It is not only the physical expansion of science departments that we work for, hope for, pray for, but for a fine integration of the abilities and achievements of all the departments. What each can give, we all may share. In this way we will give to our students the very best in a synthesis of contemporary scientific progress and far-ranging vision of the possibilities of the future."

Sister Mary Alma lives in this spirit of co-ordination and interrelation of science and the arts, and science and religion. As she teaches in lecture halls and works in her laboratories, she projects the belief that biological science is one way of exploring God's world, the belief that the full utilization of creative talent in any field is an aware contribution to God's universal plan.

St. Jeanne de Lestonnac, O.D.N.

LIFE IN THE CONVENT of the Feuillantine Sisters in Southern France was severe. These nuns abstained from all meat, followed hard and prolonged fasts, slept on board or flat-stoned sleeping platforms, and in their pursuit of spiritual serenity denied themselves virtually every physical comfort.

Into this harsh convent in the fall of 1603, at the age of forty-nine, entered Madame Jeanne de Lestonnac, widowed mother of five, all of whom were settled in marriages or convents. For years she had done works of charity and visited the poor sections of her native Bordeaux. She had worked in hospitals and taken food and money to the needy; now, freed of her familial obligations, she felt the call to go beyond this and enter a religious community.

But the physical demands on Jeanne in this Spartan atmosphere were too great to be overcome even by her tremendous spiritual belief and eagerness. Within months she became so seriously ill that the Superior was forced to return her to Bordeaux, to the home of her son. She recovered slowly, but as soon as she was able she resumed her works of charity as strongly as ever, always wondering if another approach to the religious life would be possible for her.

Two years later two Jesuit priests brought the answer. Father de Bordes phrased it directly: "As you know, Madame, we Jesuits have established schools for boys, but no order of nuns has yet begun education for girls. We have seen your work and felt your true belief and calling, and believe that you are the woman qualified to be the Foundress of such an order."

A woman matured from experience, training, spiritual make-up and drive, Jeanne de Lestonnac was perfect for the demands and responsibilities of such a bold pioneering effort.

In great joy and without hesitation, she replied, "What will be the first step, Father?"

"I believe the first move is to find some other women, responsive to this idea of teaching and at the same time eager to join you in the religious life of a new order."

In her work Jeanne had inspired many people by her acts of charity, mercy and love, her spontaneity and spiritual serenity. From these, she selected three young girls who she felt would be able to live up to the demands of the religious life. Father de Bordes chose others, and so was the foundation laid.

Building a religious order is not simple, nor is it an overnight process. The Church moves slowly, to eliminate mistakes and to leave small room for regrets of action taken in haste.

Formative work began slowly; ten postulants were selected and received. They were not able to live together as a community until the Papal approval, but they did make retreats together, and so began their spiritual bond. Jeanne found that with the help of Father de Bordes, she was to draw up the rule for the organization of her order. She spent hours studying the Rule of St. Ignatius (founder of the Jesuits) so that his ideas might guide the structure of the new order.

After the basic rule is written, it

must be submitted for the approval of the Church. First a bishop must give his support to the effort, and finally the tacit approval of the Pope has to be obtained. The Archbishop of Bordeaux, after making some changes in the rule, signed his approval, and the request for the foundation of the Sisters of the Company of Mary was given to Pope Paul V in the fall of 1606. This first order dedicated to teaching was approved in April, 1607.

As Mother Superior, Sister Jeanne gave encouragement to and inspired faith in her little community. In the first days and months there was often little to eat, too little money and no hope of finding immediate quarters for convent or school; but the spirit and drive of the pioneer were strong in her and the little community in Bordeaux became a reality. Soon there were school convents at Poitiers, Le Puy, Toulouse, Riom, Périgueux—this first venture into the education of young French girls became a snowballing success.

At eighty, bent with severe rheumatism, Sister Jeanne had one task yet to complete. The basic rule of the order had been written when it was established, but the final organization was yet to be accomplished. She spent the last few years of her long, dedicated life revising these regulations so that they might apply to the problems and difficulties which might arise in generations to come.

On her death in 1640, the Foundress left to the care of her order thirty convent schools; today schools and missions on five continents perform the same work that was begun by Sister Jeanne, proclaimed Saint Jeanne de Lestonnac three centuries later.

St. Jane de Chantal, V.H.M.

THE TIME HAD COME TO DESIGN THE HABIT; Jane de Chantal and St. Francis de Sales worked on this problem together, as they did on any decision, large or small, which confronted the new Order of the Visitations. The choice of the exact nature and cut of the veil the nuns were to wear was an important one, as the veil was the symbol of their consecrated state. Mme. de Chantal thought it should be made of crepe, but St. Francis thought a cheaper, more durable and less finely woven material would be more suitable and suggested a veiling of coarse cloth. She agreed.

There was no money to buy new fabrics, so an old and practical black traveling dress which Jane de Chantal had worn on her journey to the convent was dug out of a trunk. The dress was ripped apart at the seams, laid out and cut up, with few changes, to become the first Visitation habit, the pattern for all of the thousands which came after.

One of the nuns, Charlotte de Bréchard, was the model, standing in front of the two designers while the new headdress was being arranged and draped to hang in various folds. When they had agreed on the simplest way of arranging and wearing the veil, St. Francis took up the scissors, neatly rounded off the edges and snipped off what he considered unnecessary corners at the back. Visitation nuns of the twentieth century wear their veil now as St. Jane and St. Francis designed it that day, over three hundred and fifty years ago.

Jane Frances Fremyot, Baroness de Chantal, came from a distinguished family in Dijon, and grew up receiving the usual training and education of girls of good family in late Renaissance France. She possessed the intelligence and shrewdness inherent in the Burgundian race, and more particularly the qualities inherited from her lawyer ancestors. An attractive and strong personality, at twenty she married Christophe, Baron de Rabutin-Chantal. Theirs was an extremely happy marriage, with several children. As her

40

husband was away frequently, either at court or on army duty, she managed his estates and was a deeply loved chatelaine with a reputation for fair and beneficent treatment of all, whether tenants who worked the land, or servants in the castle, courtyards and stables.

After nine years of marriage this happiness ended abruptly in a hunting accident that was fatal to Christophe. The next eight years were spent just as unhappily as the first nine had been happy. She was forced to live, a virtual prisoner, in the home of her father-in-law, an obstinate and difficult old man. She found comfort only in her four small children and an occasional stay with her father in Dijon.

In 1604 St. Francis de Sales came from Annecy to Dijon to preach the

Lenten sermons. Madame de Chantal, now thirty-seven, listened to his teachings and philosophy and felt a strong empathy with his purpose. He too was convinced of the purposefulness of their seemingly preordained meeting. What was to be a long correspondence between the two—detailed letters concerning spiritual and practical affairs—began just a few hours after his departure from Dijon.

Their friendship and understanding deepened during this exchange of letters and their few meetings during the next seven years. The plan that Jane de Chantal eventually would enter a convent was in both of their minds. Then ideas for a new religious community gradually took shape, expressing the purpose and spiritual attitude of two great personalities who worked together in complete accord and harmony.

The plans for the congregation were first discussed in detail by St. Francis and St. Jane in 1607. Their ideas seemed to focus on an uncloistered community, doing limited charity work on the outside, open to older women and widows as well as to the young postulant. It would receive women who longed for the contemplative life although their health might not be strong enough to stand the hardships of a more austere rule (some fasted on bread and water from Advent to Easter!). They proposed to eliminate these physical obstacles and others, such as substituting the recitation of the simpler Little Office of Our Lady for the full Office. All of this meant real innovation at the beginning of the seventeenth century; in the first years of the community they were persecuted and labeled "The Order of the descent from the Cross" by those in whose opinion corporal penance and holiness are synonomous.

On Trinity Sunday, June 6, 1610, Jane de Chantal, having renounced all of her vast properties to the control of her children, entered the new convent, established in the Galerie, a small cottage on the lake a few steps outside the gates of Annecy. The beautiful orchard behind the house was reached by a covered passageway which arched over the narrow street. The beauty was all outside, for the house was bare of furniture, except for a few chairs, a table and the beds which each novice had brought; Jane had contributed her husband's army camp bed. There were no stores of food, no candles or lanterns for the

42

dark hours, and their chapel was a cellarlike room at ground level. Such was the absolute poverty in which the order was founded; and here was found complete happiness by the small group around St. Jane de Chantal.

The other two novices were Charlotte de Brichard and Jacqueline Favre. Also in the Galerie was Anne Coste, who had followed St. Francis from Geneva to become a lay sister in the new convent. They all took their full share of the domestic work and St. Francis continued their spiritual training; in his informal talks, which have been preserved to this day, are to be found a complete statement of the spirit, habits and customs of the order. Here he answered the many questions which arose in the minds of those first sisters, questions no different from those which are apt to pop up in the minds of modern novices.

Others were soon attracted to this new concept in convent life; the first three novices made their profession at the end of their first year. The congregation settled and became firm, then developed in the usual pattern; the professed sisters began their visits to the poor and the sick. Day-by-day life in in the convent began to take the general form which is still for the most part the present program of the Visitations.

St. Jane, from then on, traveled almost continuously, on horseback or in stuffy carriages, founding new communities and encouraging their superiors, negotiating real estate transactions, writing hundreds of letters, facing every sort of practical difficulty, whether it be a broken axle on a coach or the miserliness of a stubborn landowner.

By the time St. Jane died in 1641 at the age of sixty-nine, she had directly or indirectly supervised eighty-six foundations of the Visitations, creating a unity of spirit and similarity of atmosphere in the convents which lasted across the centuries, reflecting the character of simplicity in St. Francis and St. Jane de Chantal.

Sister Stanislaus, D.C.

ST. VINCENT DE PAUL told his daughters:
"Your convent will be the house of the sick,
your cell a hired room, your chapel the
parish church, your cloister the streets of the
city or the wards of the hospitals, your
enclosure obedience, your grating the fear of
God. And holy modesty will be your veil . . .
There are no nuns of whom God demands
so much as He demands of you."

Sister Stanislaus' thoughts flew back
over more than fifty years to 1883, when
she, a young nun just out of the convent at
Emmitsburg, arrived at the New Orleans
Charity Hospital.

Charity, one of the oldest hospitals
in America, had been Spanish—it had been
French—American—Confederate. It had
been destroyed by fire and hurricane. It had
seen plagues, epidemics and wars. It was
one building, small and ill-equipped; the
wards at night eerily reflected the candlelight
of the lanterns carried about by the white-
winged nuns. Five Sisters of Charity had
died in one year, of yellow jack, in these
wards, their cloister.

Sister Stanislaus was a member of
the first group of hospital-trained nurses to go
to Charity. She could remember when

people divided nurses into two kinds: the nun and the tramp. The nursing Sisters were respected, but the others, often drunken, untrained or irresponsible, were shunned.

Medicine was in a process of tremendous change and growth—and Sister Stanislaus was ready to grow along with it. The art of nursing and the science of nursing combined in her; after seeing her joy and zeal, originality and love of profession, the Superior sent the Sister to study under a world-famous surgeon in the advanced medical center in Chicago.

There she learned new operating-room techniques; she learned about sterilizing, disinfectants, asepsis, anesthetics and the necessity of keeping wounds clean. She came back to Charity Hospital with a new book, *A Nurse's Guide for the Operating Room,* which stood on her bookshelf alongside *Imitation of Christ.*

When Sister Stanislaus was not in the wards or in the operating room, she studied preventive medicine, bacteriology, the latest information and discoveries. She was the nun-nurse most wanted by doctors in surgery, she was

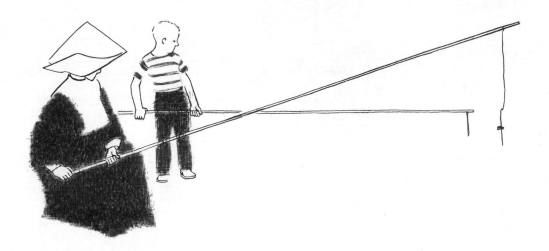

the Sister, with the pocket full of nickels, whom all of the children waited for. She was the one who, with her laughs and jokes, brought joy to the elderly in the dark, depressing wards; the tiny, blue-eyed nun who skipped her way from a sickbed through the halls and minutes later might be scrubbing up for major surgery.

Charity Hospital benefited not only from Sister Stanislaus' growing proficiency as a nurse and her increasing knowledge of surgery. She also attracted eminent doctors and surgeons to New Orleans, men who brought with them new techniques and discoveries from the medical centers of Europe and America. The entire staff of Charity was made aware of and alert to the expanding frontiers of medicine. New procedures were introduced into the operating room; and a clinic equipped for out-patient service gradually developed.

In the year 1914, a year that marked a new era in hospital administration and in the education and employment of trained nurses, Sister Stanislaus was put in charge of Charity Hospital.

She had two ambitions for Charity—to make it the most efficient institution of its kind, and to make her nurses the best in the world.

Sister Stanislaus became one of the first registered nurses in Louisiana, and she encouraged all of her nurses to follow her example; she managed to give her girls, those with wings and those with caps, a high school education. Not satisfied with this, she wanted higher education for her nurses, as well as training in every field of nursing. They began to study public nursing, physio-therapy and anesthesia.

She fought for decent wages, decent quarters, decent recreation rooms; there rose a fourteen-story home for five hundred student nurses. This building for training professional women was dedicated and named, after her death, The Sister Stanislaus Memorial.

Changing, innovating, wheedling money from individuals and governments, Sister Stanislaus gained millions of dollars for the hospital and gained a million friends for herself. She built Charity Hospital into the great institution it is today—a twenty-story monument of stone and steel and glass, a tribute to a lively and highly original nun, nurse and human being.

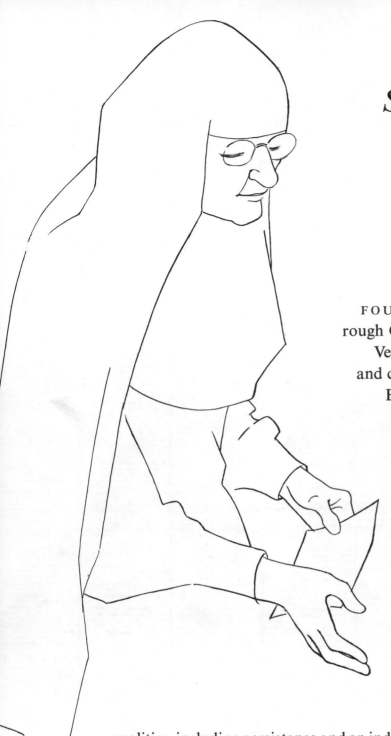

Sister Fanny Allen, R.H.S.J.

FOURTEEN YEARS AFTER he and his rough Green Mountain Boys roared out of Vermont to the shores of Lake George and captured Fort Ticonderoga from the British, Ethan Allen died, leaving his daughter Fanny a semi-orphan.

When Fanny's mother, in 1793, married for the third time, she and her husband gave Fanny the best kind of privately tutored education possible for those times in a semi-wilderness country. She was an avid reader and further extended her education in her stepfather's plentifully stocked library. Under his influence and that of the reading material in his books, Fanny developed into a firm atheist, as Ethan had been.

She inherited many of Ethan's qualities, including persistence and an independent, inquiring mind. Ironically, while the big man's thinking had led him to rebel against the Christian Church, Fanny's interest was captured by the plight of the Roman Catholics, persecuted victims of the narrow bigotry in eighteenth-century Vermont.

Her searching mind led her to an intellectual curiosity as to why, of all the sects, Roman Catholicism was oppressed by the laws of the then-independent state. Why couldn't Catholics hold public office and receive public education? Why were they condemned as disloyal, their property confiscated; why was there no one to protest this abuse?

At twenty-three, engaged to a wealthy Boston student who attended the newly established University of Vermont, Fanny suddenly announced a keen desire to round out her education by studying French in Montreal. This seemed a most logical request, as she and her fiancé were planning to travel abroad after their marriage; but was this only an excuse to learn first-hand, in a Catholic convent school, the beliefs and practices of Catholics? This may have occurred to her mother, for she insisted that Fanny be baptized a Presbyterian before going to Canada. An innoculation!

At the Notre Dame Academy in Montreal, the Sisters found Fanny quick and observing; she acquired knowledge of the religious exercises, the Sisters' teaching methods, their understanding of their pupils, their piety and devotion. Fanny admired and respected the Sisters. But because she made no secret of her unbelief, even making fun of religious services, the nuns feared for the faith of the school's young pupils and were about to send her home when a young nun to whom she had become attached won a reprieve for her.

Still she remained difficult; Ethan had given her, along with his intellect and curiosity, more than a trace of the imp. She was almost insulting in her snide remarks, which slipped out even in chapel. One day she and her young friend were arranging flowers for the chapel, and the Sister asked her to place a vase near the tabernacle, reminding her to kneel before approaching the altar.

She skipped laughingly out of the sacristy with the flower vase. Why on earth should she observe the "etiquette" of the altar when she didn't believe in the "Presence"? But her smile faded and intense emotion gripped her as she stood at the center of the altar. She simply could not move. Suddenly she fell on her knees crying, "My God! My God!" It was her first act of faith.

She was received into the Church and while preparing for her first Holy Communion, wrote home the good news. Her parents, greatly alarmed, removed her from the academy at once; but they had yet to hear the worst. When Fanny arrived home, she declared her wish to join a Sisterhood. The prejudice of puritan New England termed such a wish "voluntary suicide of the human soul"!

In an attempt to save her daughter from this suicide, Fanny's mother took her into the whirl of fashionable Eastern society, after Fanny had promised to wait a year. But after six months of trying to make her forget her "silly idea," her parents

had to let her go. She had become despondent and melancholy. Her heart was elsewhere.

Back to Montreal went Fanny Allen, she and her mother visiting convents in quest of an order for Fanny to join. They went to the Chapel of the Hôtel-Dieu, a hospital managed by a nursing and contemplative group of nuns. She joined the Religious Hospitalers of St. Joseph and made her first profession in 1808.

Sister Fanny brought her wit, intelligence and compassion to the art of nursing, and spent the rest of her life in the sick wards of the Hôtel-Dieu. All of the good qualities of her wild father had been passed on to Fanny, and her patience, warmth and beauty brought patients and other sisters alike to call her "The Beautiful American Nun."

Her influence and effect on those around her was startling. Her fiancé gave all his wealth to the poor and his services to the Catholic Church. The Reverend Daniel Barber, who had baptized her a Presbyterian, became a convert at the age of sixty-two, two years after Fanny's death, as did his wife. Fanny's virtues, they said, led them to study the religion that had persuaded her.

Then followed their clergyman son, Virgil Barber, who studied in Rome and was ordained a Jesuit; in 1823 he built the first Catholic church in New Hampshire. At the time of his ordination his wife entered the Visitation Order. Nearly all of Virgil Barber's former congregation followed him into the Church, among them a military officer who began an aggressive examination of the narrow laws biased against Catholics.

The Virgil Barbers' five children later in life became Catholics; one daughter joined the Visitations, the other three girls became Ursulines; Samuel, their younger brother, was ordained a Jesuit like his father. And the doctor who attended at Fanny's death became a convert and a Carthusian monk.

50

Ethan Allen once roared into Montreal to capture the city, only to be deported to England as a prisoner. Fanny Allen, the spirited and beautiful daughter of the "Great Infidel," rode into Montreal in quest of knowledge and became the first nun of New England, and the first American-born Sister of the order.

Thirteen Beatified Sacramentine Nuns, R.S.

On October 13, 1792, thirty Sacramentine nuns took off their habits, put on civilian disguise and lost their religious identities. For two long years they had fought the unreasoning, destructive, misspent aggressions of the French Revolution. They had refused time and again to take the oath imposed by the Tribunal and Robespierre: "I swear to be faithful to the nation and to maintain liberty and equality, or to die at my post."

This oath, which transcended their religious vows, was unthinkable; now the Sisters were forced by the Tribunal to leave the Monastery of Bollène, desecrated a few short hours later.

The persecution followed them, even in their disguise, and many were brought to the Prison de la Cure, once the parish house of the Church of Notre Dame, in Orange. The sunless, cheerless place was crowded with men and women whose only crime was their religious belief or the noble blood which ran in their veins.

The actions and expres-

sions of the Sacramentines soon made it obvious to the other prisoners that these were nuns, who offered help to the sick and solace to the lonely and frightened. Each day more victims were brought in and each morning at nine o'clock the roll call was read—the roll call of those who would die that day. Viot, the public accuser, with rolled-up sleeves, dirty waistcoat and with a sword in his hand, walked in to sound the roll call on the Seventh of July.

"Citizeness Gaillard, ex-nun!"

Sister St. Matthew was transferred to a court at the Prison du Cirque, an ancient Roman amphitheater where the executions took place every evening at six. The "court trial" of Sister St. Matthew was the same mockery of justice which characterized the times. She stood in front of the Revolutionary Tribunal and heard:

"You are an enemy of the country, you have conspired against the Republic; you have spread fanaticism and incited civil war. You have refused to take the oath. Death for Citizeness Gaillard!"

To the cries of *"Vive la nation! Vive la République!"* and to the roll of the insistent drums, Sister St. Matthew climbed the scaffold to her death.

A few days later the roll call droned out the names of Sister Pelagia, Sister Theotista and Sister St. Martin. The condemned nuns walked to the place of execution singing, in exultation, the *Magnificat*. One voice after another died out, the hymn of praise and rejoicing drowned in blood.

Next, Sister St. Xavier and Sister Martha. On July 13 Sister Madeleine . . . Sister Alexis . . . Sister Mary of the Annunciation. On the sixteenth, Sister Mary . . . Sister St. Joachim . . . Sister Aimée. Sister Mary of the Annunciation, at twenty-one, had been the youngest. The last of the nuns to mount the scaffold, Sister St. Augustine, had been taken from a sickbed at the age of seventy-four.

Thirteen Sacramentine nuns had refused to take the oath of the Tribunal and had remained true to their oath to God.

Sister Mary of St. Euphrasia, R.G.S.

WHEN SHE took her vows, an old Sister murmured in her ear, "One day you will change the formula of the vows—you are destined to do great things."

Later that day an eighty-year-old Sister said gently, "You will have so much work . . . so much work!"

Sister Mary of St. Euphrasia, at twenty-one, was destined to breathe new life and vigor into the order—the Sisters of Refuge. Begun by a missionary priest, St. John of Eudes, in 1641, it never grew or expanded during the long period of religious persecution in France. The few nuns then in the community were old and tired; they had been made timid by cruelties and were afraid of change. Sister Euphrasia was a born leader, young and full of ardor and vigor.

Within a few short years, she became Superior of the small fading community at Tours, and then with a boldness matched by her intelligence and enthusiasm, she reorganized the work and established the Sisters of the Good Shepherd.

Today we say "juvenile delinquents"; in 1835 troubled teen-agers were "wayward girls." The Sisters of the Good Shepherd received into their cloister any intractable girl who was brought by parents, by civil authorities or by prison directors who hoped that the Sisters could give help and understanding.

Said Sister Euphrasia: "The more spiritually sick our girls are, the greater should be our interest in them. The stronger their inclination to evil, the deeper should be our compassion for them. Let us then endeavor by our kind manner to strengthen the bruised reed and prevent the smoking flax from being extinguished."

She did not approach these adolescents with soft, unthinking sentiment. Rather, she used intelligence and a "built-in" sound theory of psychology. She was under no illusions about their disturbances and, often, crimes; of their hates, passions and resentments. Mother Euphrasia's formula was kindness and love, understanding and patience. She was a woman of warm heart and tender feeling, enthusiastic, spontaneous and impulsive, but behind this was realistic and intelligent control.

Under her inspiring leadership, the order mushroomed, until at her death there were more than three thousand Good Shepherd nuns working in a hundred and ten convents. The combination of warm understanding, feeling for people and her genius for organization made Mother Euphrasia one of the outstanding women of the nineteenth century. In the fields of psychology and teaching she was generations ahead of her time, in basing her treatment and therapy of problem girls on love.

Today there are ten thousand Sisters in 465 foundations throughout the world. Over twelve hundred of these Sisters are active in schools in forty-eight cities of the United States, treating and rehabilitating over eight thousand troubled teen-age girls a year.

Seven Sisters, C.S.J.

THERE WERE SEVEN. Sisters Emerentia Bounefoy, Ambrosia Anichaud, Euphrasis Suchet, Monica Corrigan, Hyacinth Blanc, Maximus Croisat and Martha Peters.

In March of 1870, they left the security of their convent in Carondolet, St. Louis, and headed west for the Tucson mission in the Arizona Territory, war grounds of the dangerous Apaches and the toughest territory in the West. Tucson, capital of the Territory, had a rapidly increasing population; the need for teachers and nurses was growing with it, and at the urgent request and plea of the Bishop in the Territory, these Sisters were sent out by the Motherhouse.

The narrow wooden cars of the Union Pacific provided the first five days of hot, dusty travel, as the iron wheels clacked along the newly laid tracks running across the plains and through the Rockies to San Francisco. A smooth sail down to San Diego on the Steamer *Arizona* gave them an easier three days; but from the coast it was to be a rough six-day trek across California, into Lower California, then into the Arizona Territory to Fort Yuma, at the junction of the California and Gila Rivers.

With Sister Ambrosia seated outside with the driver, and the other Sisters squeezed inside, the Conestoga wagon rocked along past the white post that marked the southwest boundary of the United States. The narrow trail

56

ran across mountains and over desert; the jolting wagon was unbearably hot in in the daytime sun and chillingly cold at night in the mountains. Once or twice a day a small ranch or prospector's hut would appear around a turn in the trail— a "station" which sometimes offered food and always the blessing known as water.

At the halfway point to Yuma the roadway rose sharply and unevenly to an elevation of four thousand feet. The Sisters walked, stumbled, climbed and clawed their way upward for three tortuous miles; the wagon and horses were pulled by the driver up the rocky boulder-strewn road. The altitude change was drastic for the nuns and many times one or the other would sink, breathless and with heart pounding, by the side of the trail.

Each helped the other; they struggled to the summit and finally stood at the craggy entrance to the American desert, ringed on the left by ugly mountains of volcanic rock and red sand, and on the right by a great salt lake. The two-mile descent on the eastern side was far steeper than the western slope. The trail was lined with carcasses of horses, oxen and cattle which hadn't made the climb up to the promised land of California: in one spot alone there were the buzzard-cleaned skeletons of fourteen oxen.

At the foot of the mountain they found the trail was still too tricky and dangerous to ride. The driver led his team and wagon, followed by the Sisters, who trudged on as fast as possible to reach the next ranch station for water.

The wagon left that station very early; at five A.M. they entered the desert, dangerous enough in its calm heat, and rendered even more deadly in a sandstorm. A month earlier a government wagon had been found buried in the sand; loaded with ammunition for Fort Yuma, it was several months on the desert before it was discovered. A mile away there was a stagecoach and seven passengers, also caught in the violence of a storm which had buried them. They passed a drove of horned cattle—a thousand head had died of the heat. They passed the remains of fifteen hundred sheep, smothered by a sandstorm. In places the sand was so deep the wheel hubs were covered and the Sisters walked to lighten the wagon.

At last this tired, dirty and ragged little band straggled into Fort Yuma, and was met by Tucson's Father Francisco. After only three days of rest they began the last four hundred miles, in a more comfortable wagon with plenty of provisions.

In four days they entered Apache country. Their wagon rolled past recently made graves whose crude crosses marked the remains of Apache victims. The danger of attack and massacre was with them night and day.

Seventy-five miles out of Tucson, a troop of sixteen cavalrymen joined them as escorts through the last and most dangerous part of the Territory. Another band, men from Tucson, rode up within another few miles. Some prospectors came along to gain the protection of the soldiers. The procession of cavalry, vigilantes, prospectors, horses, pack mules and the Sisters in their wagon approached Picacho Peak, the favorite ambush spot of the Apaches.

The trail wound through a narrow mile-long mountain pass, lined with grave markers. Eight cavalrymen rode ahead, followed by the Sisters' wagon, which was flanked by the Tucson vigilantes. The other eight soldiers protected the rear. Yelling wild whoops, spurring their horses at full gallop, with the wagon careening along in the middle of the bedlam, the cavalry and the men of Tucson brought the Sisters through the most dangerous part of their route, and into a fantastic reception in Tucson itself.

Three miles from town, from a cloud of dust in the trail ahead, there emerged a welcoming crowd headed by four priests on horseback. They all joined together, and as they rode eagerly toward Tucson, the ranks swelled until there were almost three thousand when they reached town. Shots rang out, lighted torches swung crazily, fireworks lit the streets. Everyone who could walk and talk was in the happy, excited crowd of ranchers, miners, far-mers, wives and children.

All the bells in the town were pealing forth as the Sisters reached the convent, from which they would give education and nursing care to the children and citizens of the frontier.

Sister Marie Louise, D.W.

IN THE CITIES of early eighteenth-century France, hospitals—such as they were—were overcrowded with the poor of all ages and description, victims of violence, famine and disease. The term hospital was virtually synonymous with poorhouse. Amidst this squalor and ignorance, at the mercy of hardened and uncaring superintendents, the poor were shut away and forgotten.

The General Hospital in Poitiers, housing more than four hundred poor, was no exception; but here the hospital chaplain was a tall, gaunt Breton missioner, Father Louis de Montfort, who dreamed of change. When nineteen-year-old Marie Louise Trichet volunteered to enter the hospital, leaving her comfortable home to live as a pauper and nurse the poor, de Montfort had the beginnings of a congregation.

The fight against the deplorable conditions in the hospital began by helping the poor devils inside to help each other; to comfort those in pain, to clean those who were helpless, to rid the place of vermin, to raise morale and bring hope. Sanitation and nursing care improved as the more active inmates, inspired by the spirit of Marie Louise and de Montfort, worked alongside them.

The dream expanded, and the Rule of the Daughters of Wisdom was written and approved; on the second of February, 1703, Marie Louise received the gray habit of the Daughters of Wisdom, the coarse woolen dress of the peasants of Vendée, chosen by Father de Montfort. Now the new congregation needed a home—a Motherhouse in which it could train novices and expand its work of mercy. There were three Sisters when that place was finally found.

It was called Long House, an old inn in St. Laurent, a small town in the

60

rugged hills of Southern France. Sister Marie Louise stood alone in the doorway; as she pushed open the door a dank, musty smell escaped from the long-neglected building. In the gloom of early evening the light of her crude lamp flickered through the rooms; everywhere it was the same—damp walls of peeling plaster, rotted floors, a few broken pieces of ill-used wooden furniture.

This was to be the Motherhouse? This was to be the school for young girls? This was the place to which parents would send their daughters as postulants? Sister Marie Louise had a supper of the coarse dry bread of the poor, and huddled by her lamp through the first long chill night at St. Laurent.

With the morning sun came renewed confidence; and with the morning sun came a young jack-of-all-trades, René Joseau, eager and willing to help the convent-to-be. With some of his friends, René within a few weeks had patched furniture, scraped walls and shored sagging floors; even a vegetable garden emerged from a patch in the unmown grass around Long House.

Sister Marie Louise and her two Sisters somehow managed to survive the poverty and hardship of the first months and years. However few, some postulants *did* come, and a school for the girls of the parish was opened . . . the congregation had taken root.

Following the foundations at St. Laurent, came Angoulême, Château d'Oléron, Poitiers, Dinan, St. Lô—until by 1750 there were twenty-one, every one distinguished by the familiar hallmark of the cross. Today, over five thousand Daughters of Wisdom teach and nurse, following the spirit of their Foundress.

Postulancy

THIS IS THE TIME when the congregation gets used to the new Sister and when she adjusts to it; it is the time when the new Sister is tested for general fitness for religious life. This period of testing is generally six months, although it may be a year.

She wears the dress of a postulant, not the habit of the novice or the professed Sister, for postulant means "one who seeks admission." Her tiny dormitory room is called a "cell" and her seat in chapel a "stall."

She finds out soon enough the work of the convent—in the laundry and the kitchen, in the orchards and gardens. In different orders, Sisters learn different tasks—baking, cooking, sewing, masonry, plumbing, carpentry, etc. Certain jobs are given to each postulant; as in any organization, a newcomer begins at the bottom. The first lessons of obedience are learned quickly. Most postulants find that a busy and brimful schedule of studies, prayer and the domestic work of the convent has been mapped out for them by the Mother Superior.

In some communities college training begins when the girl enters the convent. In every convent there is always some classwork, no matter what the order. Catholic doctrine is taught; the history of the order is taught, instilling a sense of tradition and pride in being part of it. The postulants are taught to sing Gregorian chant, and the rules and regulations of religious life in general are learned.

Day by day, week by week, the fledgling Sister begins to understand the total picture of religious life—work, play, study and prayer are woven together into a pattern of fulfillment. Gradually she feels the oneness, and the singleness, of purpose in working for the good of all, in complete dedication to God.

A postulant in any congregation or order is under constant observation and subjected to repeated tests. The Superior wants to know if she is obedient, humble, devout, strong in mind and body, and in all ways fitted for the arduous life ahead. Every day the postulant fits these into her schedule:

Mass and Holy Communion
The Rosary
An examination of conscience at noon and night
A visit to the Holy Eucharist
Reading from a book of spiritual content, usually
    selected by the Superior
Confession once a week

In each convent there are Silence Times and Silence Places. Talk must be at the right time and in the right place. Except for certain periods, there is silence most of the day, for every religious order observes silence. The work of the congregation determines its extent—a nurse or a teacher cannot keep silent during the day's work, but routine convent chores don't require conversation. The rule prevents time-wasting and allows freedom for an all-important part of the education and training of a nun.

And that is the attitude of "pray-always," the ability to concentrate on things holy in the midst of any task. Concentration on any matter, whether religious, educational or professional, is one of the outstanding characteristics of a nun. As executives and administrators, as scientists and doctors, with attaché cases or stethoscopes, Sisters have this "pray-always" attitude safely tucked away. They learn it in the early days of the convent, before going out to their assignments in the world.

Postulants may not talk to either the novices or the professed Sisters. There are five or six times a year, called fusion days, when the barriers are let down, but for the most part, postulants are a separate entity. This helps create a spirit within the group, a rapport with the other postulants; for throughout her later life, a Sister will be part of a small group always. Here, in the postulancy, in the convent, is the place to learn social limitations, to enjoy a small group, such as a family is.

Any young postulant is free to leave the convent at any time, and the congregation has the freedom to send a girl home or to suggest that she join another order which may be more suitable for her, her abilities and personality.

And, too, there is an interview which safeguards her freedom of choice; about a month before the big day of entering the order, either a bishop or his appointed delegate talks with the postulant. His job is to find out if there is any hesitancy or misunderstanding on her part, if she is doing this of her own free will. No one may ask what she said to him. After that last hurdle, and if there are no doubts or reservations, she goes into a spiritual retreat for the final eight days before the *day*.

The *day* comes—some call it Clothing Day, others term it Reception Day. It is the day when each girl receives her own habit of the order, and receives also her new name as a sister, a name usually of her own choice. The postulant has sought admission; the door stands open.

Mother Maria Alvarez, F.S.E.

AT THE HOLY GHOST CONVENT IN ROSTRENEN, a young novice attracted the attention of her Superior and teachers by her outstanding intellect. This intellect was sharpened by years of study, deepened by years of teaching and supervision; Mother Maria Alvarez matured with this experience into a brilliant co-ordinator and organizer.

During the 1902 persecution in France, more than six hundred of these Daughters saw their schools closed, and they were forced to withdraw to the Motherhouse in Bretigny, just south of Paris. Radical new plans had to be made; old plans and patterns were changed; they began anew by going to countries which welcomed them. They became missionaries.

As an advance missionary Mother Alvarez was outstanding. Wherever Sisters were asked for, she went ahead and "scouted," studied the locality and the situation, negotiated with bishops and pastors, and within two months schools opened in five Belgian towns. Other exiled Sisters went across the Channel, where England received them in High Wycombe, Olney and Ingsdon.

Teaching pioneers of the American Province arrived in New York in December, 1902; others came the following March through September, in waves of seven, six, thirty, twelve and five, and almost at once opened convents in New Haven, Bridgeport, Waterbury, Fall River and Leominster.

Late in that September of 1903 Mother Alvarez landed at the Battery with thirteen nuns. At fifty-four she was ready to bring to America the resources of her intelligence and her indefatigable activity; she had come to strengthen the young missions and to found new ones. One of the first was a school in Graniteville, Vermont, where she brought the new Sisters by horse and wagon, and installed them in their "Holy Ghost Convent."

For months on end she traveled, mostly alone, from one corner of the Northeast to the other. For the most part the mission Sisters were poorly housed and uncertain of their next meal; handicapped by a strange language and unused to the rigorous climate of a New England winter, they were badly in need of consolation and encouragment. They found both in Mother Alvarez; she built and sustained their courage, gave them advice for their teaching and left each one with a new enthusiasm for her mission.

She initiated the home-nursing program and gave it a sure and rapid start; she somehow managed to keep a reserve of French-speaking Sister teachers for the northern French-speaking parishes. She organized a postulancy to receive American girls who wished to join, where their vocation could be studied before sending them to France for their canonical novitiate.

In diplomatic jousts with bishops or in difficult negotiations with bankers, she utilized her exceptional qualities of intelligence, judgment and common sense, to say nothing of her feminine tact and finesse.

"She is a woman who understands everything," said the Bishop of Hartford.

"What a businesswoman she is!" said the director of a Hartford bank. "What a woman!"

Mother Marguerite d' Youville, G.N.S.H.

WHEN HE DIED IN MONTREAL in the hot summer of 1730, François d'Youville left a debt of eleven thousand pounds and a dishonored name to his beautiful young wife Marguerite and three children.

One by one her precious belongings went on the auctioneer's block—tapestries, paintings, silver, jewels, clothing—the tangible memories of a once happy and proud life. She sold their home on Market Place and then leased the three-story building, in which she soon installed a small shop. Marguerite stocked it with laces, threads, yarns and fabrics, and created a profitable business which supported her and the children.

Years went by, years that saw her debts paid and her store thrive; years in which gentle, compassionate Marguerite gave time, work and money for the

68

most helpless of Montreal's sick poor. She often visited the General Hospital outside the city walls to help the poor old men who had been so sadly neglected. She brought parcels of food; she mended their clothes and listened to their complaints and chatter. But she could not reglaze broken windows or repair the leaking slate roof. Once the pride of Montreal, the General Hospital was falling into ruins through disinterest and mismanagement.

With the encouragement of Father Normant, Superior of the Seminary of St. Sulpice, Marguerite took the first patient into her home. She soon found that if she wanted to increase the number of her patients and not neglect her children, her shop or other charities, she needed help. Through friendships, that help came.

On New Year's Eve of 1737, Louise Thauman, Catherine Cusson and Catherine Demers met at Marguerite's home. That night they consecrated themselves simply and privately to the service of the poor. It was the real beginning of the congregation.

Their close and unusual association began to excite comment. It was now known that blind Françoise Osseau was being cared for in the Market Place house . . . would Madame d'Youville take in more? Who was she to bring the poor of Montreal into her home and have other women nurse them? Were they thinking of taking over the General Hospital? And how could they support themselves and the poor patients? In the midst of ugly rumors and accusations, the women continued their work.

When summer came, the Market Place, the center of Montreal, came alive again. Traders came in from far outposts; drunken Indians often stumbled into the store or sat about on the steps, as they had always done. Marguerite d'Youville was their friend too. One day, through the open shutters, she overheard:

"Disgraceful! Those Indians! Where did they get liquor this time!"

"Maybe that's where the money comes from . . . maybe the Widow d'Youville sold it to them in secret, just like *he* used to . . ."

Gossip spread, rumors grew. "They sold liquor to the Indians . . . they were intoxicated most of the time . . . or at the least, a bit addled and foolish." The suspicions of friends had become public and were expressed in the insults of the mob that thronged the Market Place that

summer. The ultimate indignity happened one afternoon when the four, in plain black dresses, walked from the house toward the Cathedral of Notre Dame.

"*Voilà! Les soeurs!*"

"*Les soeurs grises!*"

The insults echoed through the Market Place. *Les soeurs grises!* The tipsy nuns!

The women walked on, tears smarting their eyes. Marquerite murmured, "But at least we were called nuns . . ."

In the midst of ugly rumors and accusations, the women continued their work. Nine years later they were formally proclaimed a congregation by order of King Louis XV; with Marquerite as Superior, the Sisters were given the management of the crumbling General Hospital. By a small miracle here, and a large miracle there, the hospital was restored over the years to its former greatness.

For nearly eighteen years Madame d'Youville and her Sisters had been called les Soeurs Grises, but the title gradually came to evoke respect rather than ridicule. The congregation was strong and was growing. The time had come to design a habit, and the Foundress chose grey—*gris* in French—as its color, and brought to the name les Soeurs Grises a beautiful meaning, the Grey Nuns.

The design of the habit was a totally original idea of Marquerite's. Practicality was its keynote; the skirt, following the old Norman style, had double box pleats and was made of camlet, a tough, closely woven cloth. The sleeves were long and full-cut, but folded back halfway up the lower arm so that they wouldn't get in the way of Sister's endless work. She also designed a dark blue-and-white-striped cotton apron which covered the habit at all times except in chapel and at formal occasions.

The Sisters worked far into the late hours of the summer nights sewing their habits. In faraway France another artisan was completing a part of their costume. Marquerite had decided that the Sisters should wear a small silver crucifix, and this silversmith engraved on each extremity of the cross a fleur-

70

de-lis, in remembrance of Louis XV. Above the Crucified was etched the symbol of the Sacred Heart. Finally a silver ring, worn by each Sister on the third finger of her right hand.

The feast of St. Louis, King of France, was a mandatory holy day. In the year of 1755 it fell on the twenty-fifth of August, the day of the first public appearance of the Grey Nuns in their new religious costume. This procession to Notre Dame was far different from the shameful exhibition of eighteen years before. As the Sisters moved quietly and unhurriedly toward the cathedral, people watched silently in the streets. Window shutters were thrown open to look out at the eleven Grey Nuns crossing Market Place.

"Les Soeurs Grises!" they exclaimed in hushed tones of awe and love. *"Les chères Soeurs Grises!"*

Blessed Julie Billiart, S.N.D.

JULIE BILLIART sat at her father's side in the low-ceilinged living room of their small cottage in the French village of Cuvilly. Suddenly a rock hurtled through the street window and crashed on the hearth, immediately followed by a pistol shot. The bullet, meant for Julie's father, narrowly missed him and nosed into the simple wood trim of the fireplace.

This severe shock to the hypersensitive young girl left Julie paralyzed in both legs, and changed the course of her life. Always a deeply spiritual person, her generous and good qualities were intensified and strengthened. Her life as an invalid led to introspection and soul-searching, and brought her closer to the Church.

The last years of the reign of Louis XVI planted the seeds of discontent and led up to the Revolution with its heedless persecution of religion and nobility. Julie's home became an underground post for hounded priests, and soon she was the target of revolutionists who called her *"la dévote."* Frightened, a family friend took Julie from Cuvilly to her Château of Gournay sur Aronde. This move aroused the fury of the citizens, who clustered in an angry mob at the gates of the château, calling out for *"l'odieuse dévote! . . . l'odieuse dévote!"* The mob was swollen by twenty horsemen who had ridden through the surrounding country, terrorizing and pillaging. Now their strident voices demanded the stake, a roaring fire and Julie Billiart.

Inside the château courtyard, friends carried the helpless Julie to an open farm cart, laid her on the bottom and covered her with a load of straw. A husky grey stallion pulled the cart through the rear gate past the angry mob, and then safely on to the nearby city of Compiègne.

Julie lived in hiding for the next ten years of the Revolution, changing her secret refuges frequently so that she would not endanger the lives of those who had given her shelter.

In October of 1794 she gained the friendship and protection of Mlle. Françoise Blin de Bourdon, who, with her noble family, had escaped the guillotine when Robespierre fell. This friendship was to last all of their lives.

Five years later the two made their last escape and went about twelve miles from Amiens to the village of Bettencourt. It was here that Julie Billiart met the Reverend Père Varin, Superior of the Fathers of the Faith. He saw in Julie not a helpless paralytic but a strong woman destined for a high mission. So sure of his judgment was Père Varin that he told Julie she should devote herself to the education of the young of France, and try to recruit women who would help her teach the uneducated, a work vitally necessary in the moral backwash of the exhausting and terrible decade of the Revolution.

Julie and Françoise returned to Amiens in 1803 and began their new

life in a large house in the Rue Neuve. With a few companions they began the exercises of a "regular life," and August 5 became the birthday of the Sisters of Notre Dame.

Julie's potential creativity was limited by her paralysis. Père Enfantin, her confessor in Amiens, resolved to obtain a miracle—the miracle of cure. Five days later Mère Julie was sitting alone in her small garden. Père Enfantin walked toward her and said slowly, "Mère, if you have any faith, take one step in the honor of Mary." Julie arose, her hand steadying herself on the arm of the chair. Then, standing erect, she took the step. Père Enfantin whispered, "Take another." She did. "A third." Père helped her sit down and smiled with great joy. "See what our Faith has accomplished!" he said softly.

Three years later Julie, Françoise and two others professed their vows to observe their rule, written for them by Père Varin. Julie became the first Superior, and drawn by her fine reputation, many novices crowded the new Institute. Soon the number in the community reached eighteen and they moved to a larger home on the Rue Faubourg-Noyon.

The Sisters were firmly established under Julie's vibrant and eager leadership and they were ready to begin their teaching—free classes for the

children of the poor. This announcement was made in Julie's characteristic open and impulsive way: she sent a novice and a postulant out of the convent into the streets. The two went in different directions, each ringing a little bell and calling aloud, "We let you know that the Sisters of Notre Dame have opened a free school for little girls! Go and tell your parents about it!" So began Notre Dame's great educational system. In 1806 the Bishop of Ghent had said to Mother Julie, "You are not intended for one diocese: Your vocation is to go all over the world."

Before her death, ten years later, nine convents had been established throughout France. Gradually this pioneer teaching order of women spread to other countries, coming to America in 1840, where the Sisters opened their first parochial school in Cincinnati, Ohio. In 1849 three Sisters of Notre Dame journeyed from that "Queen City of the West" to begin the first parochial school in the Diocese of Boston.

The Institute of Notre Dame today numbers five thousand Sisters in two hundred and fifty convents all over the world, from France to Japan, from Belgium to Hawaii.

Sister Crescentia, S.C.N.

Mycobacterium Leprae, first described by the Norwegian physician Hansen in 1874, is the acid-fast rod bacillus which spawns the horror of leprosy. In India thousands of people suffer from, are mutilated by and die from it. Many are too poor to obtain the treatment necessary to prevent its dreadful characteristic deformities. Many Indians cannot be reached, for traveling from village to village to give treatment and keep the necessary clinic records of each case is completely impractical, if not impossible, for anyone who has the responsibility of a mission dispensary. Many hesitate to seek medical examination, fearing discovery of leprosy. And yet, much of its damage can be prevented if patients are reached in time.

It was early spring of 1961 in the Nazareth mission hospital of Makameh, a thousand miles north of Kerala. Sister Crescentia had just been relieved from her long night duty and moved slowly and tiredly down the silent white corridors. She resolved to see her Superior, Sister Laurencetta, to tell her about an unorthodox but practical idea—for a "clinic under the trees," for leprosy detection and treatment. If only the people would conquer their fear and come, even those for whom it might be the last hope . . . Sister Laurencetta listened, her imagination intrigued, and she nodded approvingly at the young Sister. "It might work . . . it just might work! Go to it, Sister! Give it a try!" Sister Crescentia found her first guinea pig, Ram Dham, an Indian native in the secondary stage of leprosy. Once he had "gone over the hill" news spread rapidly among the people, and almost as soon as Sister was set up, a hundred patients a day were being treated in her outdoor clinic.

When the Indians learned that the clinic brought help and not hurt, cure and not contagion, early cases began to come to the Sisters, and for a third of these lepers a complete cure was possible. For most, there would be no deformities and the disease could be arrested.

Spurred on by Sister Laurencetta, Indian workers, using handmade bricks in solid wall and lattice patterns, put up a crude building to give cover during the approaching monsoon season. And Sister Crescentia created a plan for expert organization.

First, she gave jobs to native schoolboys every Saturday. After being scrubbed and shined, the boys squatted in teams of two on the beaten-earth floor. One made small bags and the other counted out twelve D.D.S. (Diphenyl-diamino-sulphate) pills for each bag. Other teams bagged vitamin and iron pills. For every thousand bags, the boys received a coupon, coupons which in accumulation could be traded for a prize—a bar of soap, a hat or a shirt. The incentive system paid off; each Saturday her eager helpers were on hand earlier and earlier!

Then Sister Crescentia originated a system for screening the hundreds who came to the clinic. New patients were examined by a doctor and a nurse inside the building. Those patients whose symptoms revealed no indications of leprosy were sent to the hospital out-patient clinic for further examination. Newly detected leprosy patients, as well as chronic cases, were lined up outside the small building, where six pairs of nurses handled six short lines. One of the pair checked the medical chart of each native, the other nurse distributed the two-week supplies of D.D.S., vitamins and iron pills.

So, the Sisters now plod along with twenty-five hundred patients and twelve times that many pills, for Sister Crescentia's organization allows a team of fourteen, three hours every two weeks, to handle that amazing amount. Each two-week period sees them closer to cutting down the spread of the disease, by making their patients non-infectious. By this preventive medicine, it is their fervent hope and prayer to stamp out leprosy.

Mother Theresa of the Cross Chevrel and Mother St. Augustine, O. Carm.

THE JULY REVOLUTION OF 1830, which set up the "July Monarchy" of Louis Phillipe, also created a violent upheaval in the Church. The very existence of religious orders was again denounced, as it was after the overthrow of Louis XVI and the blood bath which followed. Father Boutelou, founder of the young order which had been in existence only five years, was threatened with arrest and possible death. He fled in disguise and found refuge on the Normandy coast with trusted friends, who concealed the priest for weeks until he could be smuggled out of France.

Upon his arrival in New Orleans, so recently a part of the French Empire, Father Boutelou went directly to the bishop and gave him the first news of the Revolution and the religious persecution which threatened his congregation. Bishop de Neckere wrote to the convent asking for Sisters to come to Louisiana, where they would find safety and where they were vitally needed by the frontiers people of the new country.

For the distant and permanent mission, Mother Theresa of the Cross Chevrel and Mother St. Augustine were chosen from the small group in Tours. They left Le Havre on September 8, 1833, direct for New Orleans. Aboard a brigantine with few physical comforts, they sailed fifty-two uncertain days through the dangerous fall storms of the South Atlantic before dropping anchor in Chandeleur Sound.

A small boat bobbed in the waters fifty feet from the ship. Frantic signals and shouts told them the ship could not enter New Orleans— cholera and yellow fever ruled in the city . . . the harbor was quarantined. But the Sisters had come to stay, epidemic or no epidemic. Two black-clad figures climbed overboard by a rope ladder, clambered uncertainly into the boat and were rowed to the docks by three speechless harbor officials.

78

The Vicar General of the diocese, Reverend Anthony Blanc, met them with tragic news that brought acute awareness of the destruction of life in the city; the bishop had died of yellow fever the day before. From the terror and stench of New Orleans, the Vicar sent the Sisters through the Delta lands by the Bayou Lafourche to the tiny settlement of Plattenville, seventy-five miles west of the stricken city. There Father Boutelou was anxiously awaiting their arrival. He had readied a small house set on stilts in the bog; one room had been set aside as a chapel, and from this nucleus grew the Louisiana Foundation of Our Lady of Mount Carmel.

But the first year showed little progress. The winter of 1833–34 was a season of continuous rains, and the rough trails and roads became an impassable quagmire of mud, sand and bog; plans for building a convent and school simply had to wait. Even if there had been facilities for a school, pupils could not have traveled to and from classes. Activity was at a standstill in the too-fertile land of the Delta.

The Sisters used that winter of enforced dormancy to study their rule and constitution, and with the Father, decided what practical changes could be made to adapt to the conditions of a rough frontier country, where churches were few and far between and where the work of Sisters would be increased by the lack of resident priests. By spring they were ready for their task and restless to begin.

In Louisiana of the early 1800's the only schools for girls were boarding schools or academies for young ladies. This education was very expensive, consequently available only to the few; the many needed education too, and the time for day schools for girls had arrived.

After four years of hard work, the Sisters in the bayous achieved success, and today eleven elementary schools and six high schools in the Archdiocese of New Orleans and the Diocese of Lafayette, as well as a hospital in Thibodaux, are monuments to the great pioneers of the order.

Mother Mary Lange, O.S.P.

THE PORT OF BALTIMORE, with its fine harbor, in 1827 was quite different from the city of today. A large segment of its population was a colony of French-speaking refugees from the troubled Caribbean island of San Domingo.

Although many of these refugees were either financially independent or able to support themselves, in a city that was Southern in its sympathies and abounded in prejudices against any education whatever for the colored child, it is only too easy to visualize the hardships these people endured, the humiliations they suffered, in settling in Baltimore.

Elizabeth Lange and Marie Madeleine Balas were made acutely aware of this attitude almost from the first day they settled there. The two resolved to devote what money they had to educating Negro children and teaching them in informal but basic school classes.

Elizabeth's money, invested by her family in France, made this possible, but in that year of '27, fortunes were reversed in Paris, she heard no more from her father, and her income stopped. The school had to close.

Then Father Joubert entered their lives. Learning of the work they had been doing, this small, thin and serious French Sulpician priest came to ask them about opening a new kind of school, in which they would be not only teachers, but Sisters.

They had prayed that something would permit them to continue their work in education, and they really had wanted to be nuns, but that had been out of the question in young America, where a Negro was hardly a person, where most Negroes were slaves.

But now this priest was speaking to them about a new society, a congregation which he had the Archbishop's permission to found; and in the small, quaint chapel on the grounds of Old St. Mary's Seminary on Paca Street, their vows made in 1829 were the first to be pronounced by Negro women in the United States. Their first rule, as written by Father Joubert, reads:

"The Oblate Sisters of Providence are a religious society of virgins and widows of color. Their end is to consecrate themselves to God in a special manner, not only to sanctify themselves and thereby secure the glory of God, but also to work for the Christian education of colored children."

Today, on narrow two-lane Gun Road, which winds through Patapsco State Park, just southwest of Baltimore, sits the modern Motherhouse. Out from here fans the network of thirty-two missions and three hundred Sisters, who in the late 1950's integrated without any fanfare or fuss.

Sister Mary Ann Ida, B.V.M.

THE INTELLECTUAL LIFE CONFERENCE for college presidents was sponsored by the Carnegie Corporation and by the Fund for the Advancement of Education. Two Sisters and one priest were in that group of thirty-five which spent ten enlightening and stimulating days high in the Blue Ridge Mountains discussing Kierkegaard, Voltaire and St. Thomas; Spinoza, Plato and St. Augustine.

One of those Sisters was Sister Mary Ann Ida, an intellectual, a Doctor of Philosophy, an educator and the independent-thinking young president of Mundelein College. When she left the Chair of the Department of Philosophy to take over its direction, Mundelein, one of America's two largest Catholic colleges for women, was successful and well established. But Sister was not content to rest on the past; she looked to the future. Her challenging mind and philosophical spirit initiated a broad self-analysis of the college, in an attempt to find the answers to basic questions about the role of women in society and education and the responsibility of the institution to them.

Then, aware that a college is no better than its faculty and that the faculty must be in touch with the world, Sister focused attention on her teachers. Mundelein has more secular teachers, both men and women, than nuns. She introduced pension plans and sabbatical leaves for the lay faculty and doubled the budget for salaries. She boldly introduced laymen into many administrative positions at the college, in line with her belief that barriers between Christians, no matter whatever sector of society, should be broken down.

She released a dozen Sisters for doctoral study, another dozen for travel and study abroad (most of them on grants and fellowships) and several for post-doctoral research or stints as visiting professors on other college campuses.

She dismissed the conflicting interests of lay and religious faculty

82

members as being not a question of lay vs. religious, but conservatism vs. progressivism, age vs. youth, cultural backgrounds vs. educational background, new vs. old; in short, the age-old problem of human relations. Mundelein's faculty has a religious president who understands both sides of the problem.

As early as 1956 she helped draw up plans for the B.V.M. Scholasticate Program, a comprehensive blueprint for the educational and spiritual development of young Sisters, covering the five-year period from their entrance into the congregation until they began their work as teachers. This program favors educating young Sisters together with secular students rather than in colleges for Sisters only and believes in keeping them in some contact with "the world" even through part of their period of religious training.

Friendly, open, fast-driving Sister Mary Ann Ida is truly a nun, in, and of, the world, a well-oriented individual who has been carrying on her own grass-roots ecumenical movement for years.

Blessed Elizabeth Ann Seton, S.C.

AFTER A TWO-MONTH VOYAGE, the schooner *Pymoningo* sailed into New York Harbor early in June of 1804; young Elizabeth Bayley Seton was returning home alone. Her beloved husband, a victim of tuberculosis at thirty-seven, lay in the English burial grounds of the Italian coastal city of Leghorn. In the days and weeks of delay before her sad departure from Italy, Elizabeth had been sheltered and loved by the Filicchi family, former business associates of William Seton. In his widow, the Filicchis had seen natural goodness and humility and recognized her great spirit and capacity for understanding. Under their influence and careful guidance, Elizabeth came to know the Catholic Church in the chapels of Pisa and Florence, as well as in Leghorn. Deeply impressed by what she had seen, the young widow returned to New York torn by the struggle inside herself—a devout Episcopalian facing the strong desire to embrace Catholicism. New York, no different from the rest of the new and sprawling country, was violently prejudiced against Catholicism. The carefully groomed leaders of New York society who strolled to Trinity and St. Paul's held themselves aloof from the underprivileged, uneducated Irish and German immigrants who were the parishioners of the only Roman

Catholic church in the city, St. Peter's on Barclay Street.

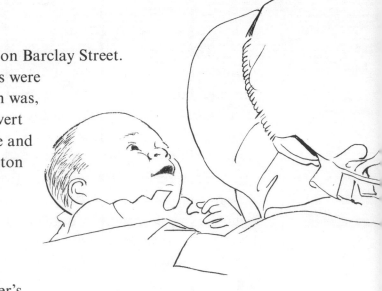

Both the Setons and the Bayleys were prominent families, and her conversion was, therefore, all the more marked. A convert accepts a new condition or atmosphere and does not turn back; when Elizabeth Seton made her change, she was, in the eyes of her friends, turning from her background and heritage, as well as her religion. Ten months after her return to New York, on March 14, 1805, she professed her faith in St. Peter's.

She soon learned the depth of feeling against her and made the terrible discovery of blind prejudice. Her two attempts to establish boarding schools for young children failed, mostly as a result of this prejudice. Her family had virtually disowned her. The Filicchis had been generous with financial help, but she could not accept their gifts much longer. Elizabeth determined at last to go to Canada, to Catholic Montreal, where she could place her children in a religious boarding school and help pay their tuition by serving as a teacher. But through Church channels, Father Dubourg, president of the newly founded St. Mary's College and Seminary in Baltimore, had learned of Mrs. Seton, and asked that she come to Maryland and start a boarding school for girls.

Leaving New York for the last time, she arrived in the port of Baltimore in June of 1808. Father Dubourg took Elizabeth and her three young daughters to a brick house on Paca Street adjoining the grounds of St. Mary's. Through its French windows, she could hear the Angelus bells which rang each day at five-thirty, one forty-five and a quarter to eight. Her two sons, ten and eleven, were scholarship students at the seminary, and when her school opened that fall, her three daughters were joined by four boarding pupils. Her dreams were beginning to coalesce—her children were being educated and cared for and she was teaching . . . at the first Catholic free school in the United States.

As the list of pupils grew, Elizabeth realized that she would need help. The hope of establishing a religious community in conjunction with the school was strong. From Philadelphia came the first recruits for teaching and for a community; one of them, Celia O'Conway, became "Philadelphia's first nun." Less than a year after beginning her new life near St. Mary's, Elizabeth and four others pronounced the vows of poverty, chastity and obedience and received their habits, designed after her simple black dress of mourning.

The progress of the small community was greatly speeded by the interest and financial help of one Samuel Cooper, a wealthy and devout Catholic. His gift of $10,000, coupled with the choice of a site for a building, led Elizabeth Seton and her companions to Emmitsburg. Emmitsburg, near the Pennsylvania border, was a small village fifty-four miles from Baltimore by a trail so rough, the Sisters had to walk the horses and wagon all the way.

They reached the village in two and a half days. Just outside, on the slope of a mountain, "St. Mary's Mount," perched a small cabin in which they spent the first few months until their "white house" could be completed. In this permanent stone house a regular community life began in July of 1809, with four new recruits, two pupils from the Paca Street school and Father Dubourg as director.

From the very first the school was a success. It was characterized by the fine caliber of the Sisters, and that caliber was set by their dedication and self-sacrifice. They suffered from the severe cold, inadequate diet and crowded quarters, and in the first six years tuberculosis took the lives of twelve young novices and Sisters under twenty-five.

Despite these hardships, more and more students and more and more novices came to Emmitsburg. It was an excellent school and a model community, run firmly by Mother Seton. Without formal training, she intuitively understood the basic principles of solid education. She was a great educator, a born teacher and an equally capable administrator. This first American Sister of Charity assigned her Sisters to teaching whatever they were able to teach; when they did not possess the qualifications she hired lay teachers for the job. Once her system was set up, she kept it running smoothly by daily classroom visits, and receiving reports from each teacher once a week.

The majority of the student body consisted of boarding students, but Mother Seton also admitted children from the neighboring St. Joseph's Parish in Emmitsburg as day students. This combination formed the nucleus of a great teaching adventure—the American Catholic parochial school system.

Elizabeth Seton was a pioneer who believed in the future of the Church in America and in her vision of social goals. Before her death in 1821 at the age of forty-seven, she had firmly established the Sisters of Charity. Her hope and optimism inspired others to carry on the work she had begun, and today there are six communities whose eleven thousand Sisters staff schools, hospitals, orphanages, day nurseries and child care centers in nine countries.

The American Sisters have achieved a long sought-for goal. In the midst of the last Ecumenical Council, Pope John XXIII bestowed on Elizabeth Ann Seton the title of "Blessed" and she will be declared, some day, the first American-born Saint.

Mother Marie Gratia, S.P.

"Taifu . . . taifu!" She turned to answer the call for doctor, doctor, as all of the Sister-nurses were known.

After setting the fracture, the Sister began to answer the ever-present questions, and a catechumenate began then and there. She was one of the original Sisters of Providence who had come to Kaifeng, China, at the request of Bishop Tacconi of Honan Province, to establish a Chinese foundation.

In 1920 Sister Marie Gratia, as Superior, and five other Sisters from Indiana became the first American community of Sisters on the mainland of China. They went deep into the heart of China, to the market towns and the peripheral farm villages; into a land of rolling wheat fields and flat wet rice fields white as snow in the harvest season, into a land of simple, sturdy people living close to the earth.

As the foundation of Sisters progressed and grew along the typical missionary lines of teaching, nursing and catechetical work, Sister Gratia formed simultaneously the Providence Catechist Society of native Chinese young women. With an eye to the future, she had the catechists trained in Shanghai in kindergarten work and at the hospitals in medicine and eye surgery. During the years the American Sisters were replaced by service rotation but Sister Gratia remained Superior.

Her wise foresight of founding a purely native Sisterhood became apparent in the troubled years ahead. Civil wars erupted between factions of war lords and political enemies; deep in the hills and mountains insurgent Communist guerillas built up bases of power. And in 1931 the Japanese moved in force into Marchuria.

During the thirties, the Sisters were surrounded by war; they did not deny their help to any wounded on the hospital trains which stopped near

88

Kaifeng. In World War II all foreigners were put into concentration camps; Sister Gratia and her Sisters, along with every missionary in China, nun and priest alike, were persecuted and jailed; but the Catechist Sisters, being natives, were not disturbed and continued their work of education and nursing among the people.

In the forties China was lost to the Communists; at the end of the war the Sisters were not allowed to re-establish themselves and in 1948 they were evacuated to Taiwan with other Americans. Sister Marie Gratia, her work in ruins, began again without any resources except missionary funds. After fifteen years, the Sisters have recovered, and a fully accredited four-year college now stands in Taichung. The Catechist Society, now an independent community under its own administration, conducts dispensaries and kindergartens in Taiwan.

With forty years of service to the Chinese people behind her, Mother Marie Gratia is the oldest American nun in years of service in China and the only survivor of the original band of six. A few years ago, at her convent on Taiwan, she was given a citation written in ancient Chinese and beautifully bound in brocade, thanking her for her long dedication to the education of the Chinese people. In recognition of her valiant efforts, she has been honored by her Superiors in America with the personal title of "Mother," a title usually reserved to the Superior-General.

Sister Anna Marie, S.S.F.

THE SUMMER VACATION after the first year of novitiate in 1930 was spent at St. John Berchman's Girls' Home. Sister Anna Marie, a rather frail young girl of twenty, was a novice in this order which had been founded approximately twenty years before the Emancipation Proclamation, to educate and help Negro women and to instruct slaves.

The novitiate used the third floor of the large home, its spacious, well-equipped and freshly painted dormitories, recreation hall and chapel. In the Home there were seventy-five girls of all ages, from a few days old to perhaps eighteen. There were nurse-assistants, service and kitchen help, and the Novice Mistress. The setup was designed to give a gradual approach to contact with children and other seculars, a near-approach to mission work.

Young Sister Marie gave every ounce of her intelligence, humor, sensitivity and *joi de vivre* to her vocation. She studied institution work, visited the children and the nursery, asking questions about the work: the methods used for inducting new children who were old enough to feel the loss of their home and parents, plans for their life after leaving the orphanage, about adoptions, about deciding upon official names for babies of unknown parentage or for unwanted babies.

But her strongest interest was in the older girls—the good that could result if they were sent out to parochial elementary schools; how the exchange of talk about six or seven schools would brighten up their lives when they returned to the Home each day; how the personality of the girls would improve if they did not have to wear uniform institution clothing every day; how various colleges of the city could send drama, speech, athletic and music seniors to conduct Saturday classes for the children; how the older girls could go on to high school at St. Mary's Academy.

Full of desire to help them, Sister Marie asked permission to spend

90

extra time with a group of these girls. She
created informal "get-togethers" and asked
about their future plans, and how they expected
to achieve their goals. For some there was
a dead end at the point when they would
leave the Home, and for most the only
prospect was to go into domestic service.

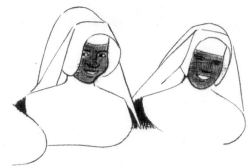

Then Sister encouraged them, and
explained that the professions were for them as much as for anyone else if they
had the ability, courage and patience to investigate and prepare for them. Her
words took root— every one of the girls to whom she spoke completed high
school. Some married, became mothers, one is a registered nurse and wife of a
doctor, one a social service graduate, and three became Sisters of the Holy
Family.

This period became Sister Maria's first and only mission. After her
final vows, before her first mission as a Professed Sister, tuberculosis struck.
She had always had an extraordinary devotion to St. Theresa, the Little
Flower, and coincidentally, when she also was twenty-four years and three
weeks old, she died on her feast day.

Had she lived past her youth, she would have been a tremendous force
in the Holy Family Sisters. Every one of her suggestions made during that
summer at the orphanage were adopted within a year after her death. But in
her enthusiastic giving of life and in her courageous acceptance of death, she
was an inspiration to all around her.

Mother Mary Carmelita, R.S.M.

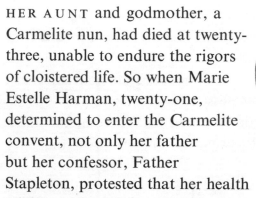

HER AUNT and godmother, a Carmelite nun, had died at twenty-three, unable to endure the rigors of cloistered life. So when Marie Estelle Harman, twenty-one, determined to enter the Carmelite convent, not only her father but her confessor, Father Stapleton, protested that her health might not be strong enough. Father Stapleton also felt that her abilities and inclinations would be used to better advantage in an active community. She entered as a postulant with the Sisters of Mercy in Baltimore and six months later became a novice, Sister Mary Carmelita.

The Father had been right about her—she was destined for an active order, and destined also to make that order even more active! After eighteen years of teaching and hospital administration Sister Carmelita became Mother Superior in 1923.

Shortly after, she received an urgent request from the Sisters of Mercy in St. John's, Newfoundland. An epidemic had taken the only graduate Sister nurse in the new St. Clare's Mercy Hospital. Sister Carmelita left immediately for St. John's, taking with her an experienced nurse, Sister Terista.

She kept in close touch with the Sisters in the ranks, and always tried to choose the right Sister for the right assignment. She had brought Sister Terista to St. Clare's for what turned out to be an eighteen-month tour of duty. Mother Carmelita then took two Newfoundland Sisters to enter the Mercy Hospital School of Nursing, and when these Sisters graduated and returned to St. John's, others continued the thread of training at Baltimore.

In the same year of her election she supervised extensive remodeling of the convent; flagrant fire hazards, the rambling wooden verandas girding the buildings, were torn down. Reinforced concrete porches, supported by sturdy columns, replaced the originals. From a hassle with the contractor, her attention was turned to the summer rest home for the Sisters at Mercy Cliff Sea Isle, in New Jersey. It was in sad need of repair, and somehow she managed its renovation and enlargement to give more Sisters an opportunity for a short period of rest in the summer months by the shores of the Atlantic.

The schools on Mount St. Agnes, also the location of the Baltimore community, had become overcrowded and many of the convent buildings were outdated. The time was ripe for action and Mother Carmelita never hesitated to act. McAuley Hall, the present main building of St. Agnes College, rose, stone after stone, beam after beam. Even before it was finished the need for a new plant to service the Hall became evident, and Mother Carmelita supervised its construction, completing another achievement of the Sisters of Mercy.

She then turned to the restaffing of three parochial schools in the Archdiocese. Becoming aware of weakness in the teacher-training program, she brought to fruition a seed planted in earlier years and planned a system for Sisters to obtain teacher's certificates, to complete college work and follow courses leading to higher degrees.

In the eighty years since the establishment of the order, America had reached out and found its boundaries, and the Sisters had followed and matched in growth; there were Motherhouses in many of the dioceses. Every Motherhouse, with its dependent branch houses, had its own governing body and functioned independently of other communities of Sisters of Mercy. It had gradually become evident that this sprawling system had to be contained, that there had to be a central government with uniformity of rules and customs, under one revised constitution.

The problem was placed in the capable hands of Mother Carmelita. With the technical advice of several professors of canon law, she pored over the thousand details involved in preparing the petition of change for Rome. Less than two years later, the Papal Decree was issued; a Decree uniting the

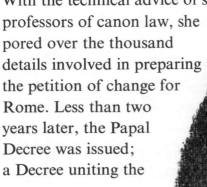

communities into one Religious Institute under the government of one general Superior. In August of that year Mother Carmelita was elected the first Superior General.

And she was off again—she called meetings of the Mothers Provincial, of the Procurators Provincial, of the Mistresses of Novices of the different provinces, to discuss ways and means of creating further uniformity and then maintaining it in the years of future growth. She kept up quite a pace—in each of her two six-year terms as Mother General, she visited all of the more than four hundred houses of the Institute.

Keeping in close touch with all of the Sisters was her wise prescription for a sound and progressive order. To draw them closer together, she conceived the publication of a news magazine for circulation among the Sisters, to let them know one another's activities and the activities in the General Motherhouse. The *Generalate Quarterly* has brought knowledge and information to thousands of Sisters.

Her drive and energy were fantastic. During her time as Mother General there were hundreds of projects to which she gave approval and encouragement: three new hospitals, four taken over from other management; homes for nurses; colleges for women; a home for the aged; improved staffing of parochial schools—on and on and on.

Even after her terms as Mother General, when she was elected Mother Assistant General, she was ever alert to the needs of the sick, the poor and the ignorant. When she died, after almost sixty years as a Sister, she had seen the Institute grow to sixty-five hundred members, conducting ninety-three hospitals, two leprosaria, fifty-eight schools of nursing, nine colleges, one hundred and four high schools, four hundred and six elementary schools, eight catechetical schools, five summer camps, seventeen residences for businesswomen, twelve child-caring homes and twelve homes for the aged in the United States, British Honduras, British Guiana and the British West Indies.

Sister Mary Madeleva, C.S.C.

SISTER MARY MADELEVA RETURNED to Saint Mary's College at Notre Dame in 1934, to become its president. The dismaying depression years of the thirties rolled by and we rushed toward the tragedy of Pearl Harbor. In the fall of 1941, at a teachers' conference at Saint Meinrad's, Indiana, Monsignor Morrison stopped Sister Madeleva in the corridor.

"Sister, will you receive Negro students at St. Mary's?"

"Of course we will, Monsignor."

"Good. I have someone in mind."

Saint Mary's had never received Negro students because no Negro had ever applied. Several times Sister Madeleva was asked by the Superior General, a Virginian with a deep Southern heritage, just what she would do in the event of an application by a prospective Negro student. Her unvarying answer was acceptance of course, as long as she qualified academically.

An application came to the admissions office early the next spring, an application for admittance as a resident freshman. It was accepted and the first Negro was enrolled at Saint Mary's. Sister Madeleva had decided to minimize and play down this happening, which was bound to arouse inevitable objections. She knew that the right moment for its communication would come. Nothing had been said to either faculty or students; she waited.

Baroness Catherine de Hueck, founder of the Friendship Houses in New York, Chicago and eastern Canada, an ardent champion of the Negro and a forceful exponent of integration, came to deliver a series of lectures. One day in the Great Hall, a group of students had crowded around the Baroness after a lecture, pressing her with questions and thoughts, voiced by girls mainly from the South. Troubled, they asked what they could do to overcome the instilled prejudices and teachings of past generations.

"If you mean what you say, you will simply receive and welcome Negro girls to your college . . . try sincerely to make them feel a part of St. Mary's," came her resolute reply.

Sister Madeleva's right moment had come. She made the first announcement of Saint Mary's policy on the racial issue, informing these students of the acceptance of a Negro girl for freshman residency in the fall.

From faculty, parents and alumnae came most articulate forms of protest, doubt or approval. But the afternoon of September, 1942, brought Freshman Registration Day, and a reception and tea to welcome students and their parents. Into the lounge walked two handsome women with a beautiful young girl—three generations—grandmother, mother and daughter, each with her own particular emotions and memories on this day.

Conversation stilled for a moment, and then a faculty member hurried over to greet them, a teacher who was having difficulty in visualizing integration at conservative Saint Mary's.

"We are so happy to have you . . . and what is your name, my dear?"

"Carmelita Desobrey."

The gentle Sister put her arm around the first Negro student, saying, "Carmelita, Carmelita, you are so welcome to Saint Mary's and to our Holy Cross family."

Integration at Saint Mary's had begun.

Françoise Perreton, S.M.S.M.

FRANÇOISE PERRETON WAS NOT A MARIST SISTER. In a sense she was more, for she planted the seed of the order, more than ten years before its flowering.

Françoise, the daughter of a professional soldier (and she proved to have inherited his courage), was a middle-aged woman leading a sheltered and contented life in Lyons. This contentment was dissolved when Pauline Jaricot, the inspired Foundress of the world-wide Society of the Propagation of the Faith, set Françoise afire with enthusiasm for mission work. Her ardor had plenty of time to cool, for she found very little support for her idea of giving the remainder of her life to the natives of a remote tropical island, natives who might be friendly, hostile or cannibalistic.

For many long months she pleaded with the Marist Fathers in France to let her join the missionaries in Oceania—that vast area of South Pacific islands to which the first mission group of priests had gone just nine years before. Foreign missions of the monasteries of Europe were still a rarity and women missionaries were unknown in 1845.

The Fathers gave in to the overpowering enthusiasm of the woman who said her call was truly from God, and at last agreed. The captain of the ship outward bound for the islands at first refused to have a woman aboard, let alone sail the long and dangerous voyage halfway around the world. But no captain could for long dissuade a woman of her caliber; on November 15 the ship weighed anchor in Marseilles with Françoise Perreton aboard. It was just six months after the massacre of St. Peter Chanel in Oceania.

The course of the *Ark of Alliance* was charted across the southern Atlantic to the port of Montevideo, through the perilous Straits of Magellan to Valparaiso, west across the blue Pacific to the Marquesa Islands and to Tahiti. The final leg of the incredible ten-and-a-half-month voyage was the run from Tahiti to another of the Society Islands.

The *Ark* dropped anchor in the calm waters off Wallis Island. Missionaries and natives alike waited quietly on shore, curious to see this brave woman who had dared to give up everything and come to the South Pacific. She brought the first news from Europe in over a year to the eager priests; a precious packet of mail and sorely needed medical supplies came in the dinghy which rowed her to shore.

A small hut was ready for her—a woven reed mat on the earth was her bed, an upturned crate was her table, and banana leaves her china. As simple as the hut was her food—bananas, fish, yams, taros and coconut milk. Her new life began.

This relative poverty did not bother Françoise. She overcame the language barrier; she grew used to the mosquitoes, insects and reptiles, and to the hurricanes and typhoons which bent low the palms that ringed the island.

The awful thing to bear was the isolation. She had known that a lonely island was, of course, isolated, but here she not only was without contact with the outside world, she had none with human beings in her island world. The priests had to keep apart from her, for fear that the natives would harbor wrong thoughts about their relationship. She had not even the privacy of

the confessional—Françoise had to stand on one side of the stream which separated the Fathers and her, and call out her sins to the priest standing on the other side.

The years went by, her lonely exile broken only by an occasional ship bringing news from France or tragic but proud bulletins of violence and hostility in the Marist missions to the South—in Tonga, Samoa, New Caledonia and the Solomons. The news of martyrdoms and of gallant pioneer accomplishments caused ambivalent reactions in Françoise Perreton. She felt pride in the progress of the missions and at the same time an almost overpowering emotion of frustration; frustration of her own unfulfilled mission desires.

She did not realize that hers was a real martyrdom too. Not by torture, disease or a quick knife thrust, but a long, slow martyrdom of loneliness, a martyrdom of apparent failure. And yet she did not fail, she was successful beyond her dreams, beyond the accomplishment of a few years. She was a pioneer in a far different way; she proved that a civilized, delicate woman could stand the tough life of the Pacific missions. Under the worst possible circumstances she had proved it.

Her life on the remote Pacific island was instrumental in the founding of a congregation of women expressly for the Marist missions. Sisters trained in crafts and language, in nursing and teaching, with full knowledge of what lay ahead—these were the Marist Sisters.

So after almost twelve years of solitary existence, the prematurely aged Françoise was joined by three Marist Sisters, who between them gave

eighty-six years of mission service. In four years seven more came; they all came with no thought of return. In those days when a Sister went to her mission it was for life, working two-by-two in uncertainty of what the next day would bring, completely out of touch with civilization except for the ship which appeared once or twice a year.

Françoise Perreton had brought something new into the Church: Sisters who were out in the front line of duty, on horseback, in a dugout canoe, in a hut on a hurricane-swept island—Sisters without a cloister, creating new frontiers. The first woman missionary in the South Pacific, she cleared the path for hundreds of Sisters who would follow her in the years ahead.

Novitiate

IN HER NEW HABIT OF THE ORDER, the new Sister leaves the ceremony in the chapel to begin a lifetime of service. But there is still a period of training, the novitiate of either one or two years, before she will take the vows of a Professed Sister.

This habit—the distinguishing dress—has become a symbol of what the nun stands for: dedication and trust. The habit identifies her as a part of the tradition and history of her order as well as binding her to its future. The novice is taught the meaning of the holy habit, and she is taught to wear it properly, for a vocation doesn't assure her that she will know how to arrange or wear the habit automatically.

Her new name further identifies the Sister with the order and those within her group, as she leaves the old identity outside the convent walls. From now on, her world is the world of her work, her fellow Sisters, the community and service of God.

One year of novitiate is a must by canon law, but many sisterhoods require two years. Right away, in that brand-new habit, the Sister plunges into a heavy schedule of spiritual training. This is the time for spiritual formation, of concentration. Quite often, no visitors are permitted during this year; or if they are, very few.

This is the year the novice studies herself in relation to the order and concentrates on adjustment to her spiritual life, present and future. She is kept as free as possible from distraction, whether from the outside, or from convent chores and most secular studies on the inside. By far the majority of her classes are concerned with the study of the constitution of the order, of Christian Doctrine and the Bible, particularly the New Testament; there is further practice in Gregorian chant. It is time of complete concentration on learning to be a Sister.

Study, prayers, work, study, prayers and still more study fill each day. As in learning anything, it requires constant effort, repetitious effort; then one day, a new plateau is reached—a new plateau of understanding. The phrase the "Common Life" begins to mean something. The Common Life of the convent means everyone has a common schedule for the day. Sharing the same morning hours of rising, sharing prayers in chapel, sharing the same food in the refectory, sharing the identity of the habit, sharing the same type of "cell"; these patterns bring comfort and provide happiness.

The familial spirit of any congregation is strong, even though it varies from order to order. In the novitiate year this spirit sinks in—a strong sense of belonging, of being a member of a family, fills the young Sister.

This Canonical Year also includes learning to recite the Office—the Little Office of the Blessed Virgin, or the longer Divine Office. The Office is composed of readings from the Scriptures, psalms, biographies and writings of the saints, etc. They are said in Latin and in English; they are chanted and sung. Following the idea of the Common Life in a most practical way, the novices say the Office in common during their Canonical Year. Later on, as Professed Sisters, they say it privately. The little black book (the Breviary) which you may see a Sister reading in a bus or in a doctor's waiting room, contains the Office.

But all work and no play makes a poor novice. Just because they wear religious habits does not mean that novices spend the whole day on their knees. Relaxation during this strenuous year is very important to proper religious formation. Novices enjoy many games which any young women like; they are encouraged to play tennis, badminton, basketball and baseball, as well as enjoying the quieter pleasures of checkers, chess, card games and dramatics. The purpose of careful novitiate training is to produce a well-rounded human being, an individual secure in her religious foundation.

The same freedom of choice is open to the novice as to the postulant—at any time the novice may leave, or the Sisterhood can request that she leave or change orders, for mutual benefit.

At the end of this Canonical Year, a Sister has a pretty good idea of the years ahead. She cannot see her future field of dedication perhaps, but she knows the schedule of the convent, the feeling of the Common Life and the spirit that pervades the order. Her decision to remain has been reached; but again, as in the postulancy, the bishop or his delegate has a meeting with her shortly before Profession Day. If all seems well to him, a certificate to that effect is issued to the Superior. Following this, the Sister goes into another spiritual retreat for eight days before Profession Day.

Profession Day—the day the novice takes her vows and becomes a Professed Sister . . .

In the chapel the novice kneels before the Mother General. Her voice strong and clear, the Sister makes her vows of religion, vows which are a public act just as are those of marriage. She says, in effect:

BY THE VOW OF POVERTY, I GIVE UP MY POSSESSIONS.

BY THE VOW OF CHASTITY, I GIVE UP MY HEART'S LOVE

TO GOD ALONE.

BY THE VOW OF OBEDIENCE, I PROMISE TO DO HIS WILL

FOR ME AS SHOWN BY MY LAWFUL SUPERIORS.

Having made her solemn vows, the newly professed nun is given a crucifix and the black veil which replaces the white veil of the novice. Then she receives a ring, placed on the third finger of her right hand (in some orders it is worn on the left) as a symbol of her lofty espousal.

This is called Temporary Profession, made for a short period of time—one year, two or three. Her vows are renewed at the end of that time, for still another year, two or three. A Sister may leave at the end of any of those periods. But every Sister intends a life-long dedication when she takes her first vows. She means "for life" when for the first time she publicly makes her promise to live the more perfect life.

At some certain time—it varies with different orders—say, six years, a Sister takes Final or Perpetual Vows, and from then on is bound to her order in complete dedication.

Sister Mary Theodore, O.S.F.

SISTER MARY THEODORE, a novice of nineteen, took her first train ride, a fifty-mile trip from the Franciscan convent in Milwaukee to St. Lawrence School, a two-room country school, to teach grades one through four.

Across the lane, just below the brow of a hill, was the Franciscan St. Colleta School for Backward Children. Here Sister lived and here she came to know the retarded boys and girls who needed special care and training. Here she learned that a large percentage of mental retardation is caused by physical accident to the child, that it could have happened to her, or to any of her thirteen brothers and sisters, or to anyone.

Four years later Sister Theodore took her lifetime vows and volunteered to teach at St. Coletta's, the oldest and largest Catholic school specializing in work with the mentally handicapped. When it was founded in 1904 by four Sisters pioneering in special education, basic elementary schooling for the retarded was practically unknown. These children were put into asylums or hidden away somewhere by families who simply did not understand and who could not bear the ugly whispers of society.

As late as 1930, when Sister Theodore began her work, most facilities, whether state or private, were shamefully inadequate because there was still widespread misunderstanding of the cause of mental retardation. Shame and stigma were attached to the family of such a child.

In staff conferences and through professional reading, Sister Theodore learned that the retarded child is a child who lacks the potential to develop even average mental ability, whether this potential was destroyed by injury or disease before birth, at birth, or in the child's very early years; and that it is not a disease, nor is it any form of mental illness or insanity.

Through careful and close attention to individual needs, the different child is made less different. He cannot be made normal, but he can be made better and more adjusted. This retarded child may sometimes ask the question "Why?"

106

One eight-year-old, named Tom, his height that of a five-year-old and facially scarred, hung around the classroom after school to help Sister. Shuffling the erasers in the blackboard trough, he said quietly, "Sister, why did God give me such a funny mouth and poor talk, and big ears?"

Sister Theodore drew in her breath sharply. Then turning, and looking into the boy's eyes with kindness and understanding, she said gently, "Well, maybe God knew that you could take them better than some other little boy." A twisted, grateful smile brightened Tom's face.

Another time a small girl asked, "Why is the school called St. Coletta's School for *Backward* Children? We don't walk backward!" The school became St. Coletta's School for Exceptional Children.

An understanding teacher is a vital person in the life of the retarded child, who needs every help a devoted and resourceful person can give. Sister Theodore, in her dedication, has given over thirty years to realizing the highest potential for these children. She has seen progress and been a part of it: intelligent informing of the public and parents, early recognition and diagnosis of mental retardation, and the awakening of the medical profession to the existence of over 1,600,000 retarded children of school age in this country.

107

Sister Maria Soledad, S. de M.

IN THE SUNLESS SLUMS OF MADRID the hovel of Manuel Torres, dairy-man, squeezed crookedly between the other cell-like sheds lining the open sewage gutters on Low Flower Street. Here, on December 2, 1826, was born one more child of the slums, another bitter fruit of overcrowded housing, non-existent sanitation and ever-present malnutrition. She was named Vibiana Antonia.

At fifteen, if her appearance was ordinary, if her constitution was weak, her compassion was extraordinary and her concern for the people of Madrid's slums was strong. Tiny Vibiana visited the sick, brought food carefully saved from the meager Torres table, and spent hours giving companionship, under-standing and encouragement to those of little hope.

When she was twenty Vibiana Torres applied at the cloistered Domini-can convent to be accepted as a white-veiled Sister, a Sister dedicated to domestic chores rather than to the choir. She was accepted, but as the rule of the community restricted the number of Sisters in the convent, she had to wait.

Across the city, in the poor suburb of Chamberi Plaza, Father Michael Martinez was with two old friends. For a long time he had thought of the many cases of illness which could be treated only in the home, rich and poor alike—of the need for "visiting nurse" Sisters. The conversation of the three men centered on the illness of the governor's daughter, and this conversation sud-denly crystallized the Father's thoughts. He stopped abruptly in their walk and said to his startled friends, "There must be a congregation of Sisters to nurse in the homes of the sick. I shall go to the Cardinal in Toledo."

108

The Cardinal was most responsive and quickly gave permission for the foundation of a new community, Sisters, Servants of Mary, and Father Michael began his search for the nucleus of seven young women of Madrid. Vibiana was the last to be admitted, after Father Michael overcame his doubts of her physical ability to withstand the hardship of living in a new congregation and nursing the sick. She was also the last to receive the habit, and was named Sister Maria Soledad.

These Sisters suffered great poverty and privation in their new life. Many times their daily meal was garlic soup and dark bread. In the hovels of the poor and the mansions of the rich the Sisters worked long hours, long nights at the bedside of the sick and the dying, and became known affectionately as the "Angels of Mercy."

Over the years civil persecution, revolution and poverty created many changes in the congregation. At the nadir of despair, when the very existence of the community was in danger, Sister Soledad was named Superior. Single-handedly she brought it back to life and inspired patients rich and poor, authorities civil and military. Her charity for the poor knew no limits. During two dreadful cholera epidemics the Sisters were the only ones permitted out of quarantine, to risk their lives in answering desperate pleas for help.

Sister Soledad sent food, blankets, clothes, anything she could get, with the Sisters who were caring for the destitute—and always more came, from unknown benefactors, to the convent door. She began to open new houses throughout Spain. The community began to be better known and more vocations came.

This child of the slums, so familiar with all of its meannesses, tried all her life to bring light and hope into those dark corridors of filth and disease.

All Madrid paid her honor when at last she could fight no longer.

Sister Marietta, M.S.V.

IN THE LOMBARDY REGION OF ITALY, the sleepy little town of Limone nestled on the shore of misty Lake Garda, in the foothills of the Alps. Just five years after he had realized his dream of creating the Missionary Sisters of Verona, Monsignor Camboni, a native of the village and a great African missioner, returned to his birthplace to be consecrated as a bishop.

This inspiring man captured the mind and imagination of fifteen-year-old Marietta, a girl full of energy, generosity and high spirit. In school, her teacher had often read letters from his missioner brother in Africa, and the young girl had been fascinated by his stories of the country and its people. Now as she listened to the Bishop and his far-reaching plans to educate and help the Africans with his community of Missionary Sisters, Marietta knew that she was called.

With three other girls she joined the novitiate at Verona, a scant twenty miles southeast of Lake Garda. Two years later the Bishop and a pioneer group of Verona Sisters sailed for Alexandria. As she was only seventeen, Sister Marietta was assigned to Cairo, and the older Sisters went

110

deeper into Africa. Some years before, Bishop Camboni had founded an orphanage and asylum for freed slaves, and here Sister Marietta began her mission work. This meant long hours of teaching language, customs and hygiene; and spending long hours working in the medical clinic.

After five years of exhausting work and two bouts with dysentery, Sister Marietta was forced to return to Italy. But soon, restless and impatient, she was back in Africa, this time to Aswan, an outer mission on the banks of the Nile.

Day after day, year after year she served—she learned the languages and dialects in Egypt and Ethiopia, she learned to know the people, and they came to love and trust her. To her they brought their problems and their sicknesses; tuberculosis, dysentery, yaws, beriberi, burns, and snake bites waited in line outside the clinic door each day.

She taught Christianity too, and baptized thousands of children and adults. There seemed to be no end to the energy and devotion which she gave out in great doses to the people. She was able, too, to teach and help to an extraordinary degree the young Sisters who arrived from the Motherhouse. Her long experience gave her deep understanding of the African people, which she passed on to those youngsters who were beginning their mission life.

But even Sister Marietta's energy had its limit—she died in the African desert at ninety-three, after an incredible service of over seventy-six years as a missionary.

Sister Mary Borgia, W.S.

THE FIRST DOCTOR TO BECOME A WHITE SISTER was a young English girl who had been converted to Catholicism by her fiancé while she was studying medicine. After receiving her degree, Frances Wilkinson interned at a hospital in northern England.

There she attended a retreat preached by a White Father. He did not speak directly of mission work, but he somehow projected a missionary spirit into his talk, and the young doctor was profoundly moved. For some time she had been stirred by strong feelings of a vocation and now came the realization that in combining her medical training with missionary work she was ready for the convent. She terminated her engagement and entered the postulate of the White Sisters at Heston.

In 1936 there were very few English White Sisters and no novitiate in England; so it was that in May of the following year she received the white habit of a novice in Belgium, and took as her patron Saint Francis Borgia and as her name, Sister Mary Borgia. Her second year of novitiate was spent at the North African Motherhouse near Algiers and Sister Mary Borgia made her first vows in May of the fateful year 1939.

One of the largest White Sister hospitals in North Africa is at Les Attafs, one hundred and fifty miles west of Algiers in the Cheliff plains. There Sister Borgia was sent and there she worked as a

ward nurse until a few months later when World War II exploded. The surgeon in charge of the hospital was called up for active service and Sister Borgia replaced him.

Notre petit docteur, as the Sisters called her, took over with eagerness and anticipation. The demands were heavy, the responsibility great, but she met them with superior medical skill and hard work. Even though this work left her little freedom from duties, Sister Mary Borgia always found time to help her Sisters in the humble household duties. If she had a Sunday free, she could usually be found at a kitchen chore, while more than once the older Sisters found their shoes had been polished for them when no one was looking.

An eye clinic was opened by the White Sisters in Algiers and Sister Borgia was appointed there so that she might widen her experience in treating the many chronic eye diseases prevalent among the Arabs. Although many East African missions were asking for the new Sister-Doctor, wartime restrictions kept her in Algeria for three years.

The war went on. The Americans landed on the coast of North Africa; Montgomery and Rommel struggled for mastery of the desert. Algiers was frequently bombed and the clinic staff was forced into the cellars beneath the clinic during the raids.

On Sunday, November 22, 1942, there was a long afternoon raid followed by a short "All clear." The sudden calm tempted six Sisters to go up to the chapel for the evening prayers. They were kneeling before the altar when the bomb fell.

It was not a very big bomb; it went straight through the upper stories of the house and exploded in the chapel. Six missionaries, the entire staff of the eye clinic, in their prime productive years, were wiped out. Sister Mary Borgia, thirty-one years old and professed just three years, was killed instantly.

Sister Marie Alicia, I.C.M.

"AFTER THE NOVITIATE WAS OVER, I was offered the choice of continuing my study of music, or going into social work. As I could not see myself as a missionary teaching piano for the rest of my life, I chose social work."

And more than choose it, this twenty-six-year-old Belgian, Sister Marie Alicia, went after it. Three years of concentrated study and field work at the Catholic Social School in Brussels gave her a degree in social work. Before going on to her mission station in Dominica, she was sent to the provincial house in New York to study English, and to Illinois, Wisconsin and Washington to observe the social work methods in the United States—child welfare work, family case work, the operations of prisons and institutions. It was in America that she had her first contact with credit unions, which provide a common pool of savings from many contributors, from which the individual contributor, or depositor, can draw when he is in need of help.

On her way to her mission, she was sent for a final "briefing" in Jamaica for ten days, to observe social action in a West Indian setting—to get a feeling of the people and their customs, habits and attitudes—before starting her own work. She investigated the island, inquired at the parish credit unions, explored the plantations, visited the homes of the people, and then continued east across the Caribbean to Dominica.

Dominica—a craggy, mountainous island with occasional black sand beaches along its rugged shore line—lying between Martinique and Guadeloupe in the Antilles.

Sister Alicia watched the men on the banana plantations; watched them at the docks loading the ships with cargos of fruit; watched the women trying to feed the children with too little, always too little, in poor shacks that offered no protection from the torrential rains and squalls which relieve the tropical sun and enrich the soil. She saw the children, oh, so many, their bellies swollen by malnutrition.

Sister Alicia had prepared for this mission; five long years she had studied, observed and worked. She had learned in Jamaica that the most urgent need in the islands was the establishing of the principal of self-help, of the credit unions, because they, more than anything else, could lift the people's standard of living. Now was the time to act.

She organized the first Dominican credit union, and taught the people how to build up savings from their meager earnings, for future needs. But they also needed immediate help. At the same time, she planned services to benefit the communities right away; she initiated the war against malnutrition with a hospital, a surplus food plan and a public health program.

Over the years Sister Alicia kept on studying; never isolated from the outside world, she kept abreast of improved social work techniques with a six-month U.N. Fellowship and courses and seminars at Teachers College, New York.

Today this social worker Sister is Director of the Dominica Social Center, which includes a day nursery, pre-schools, a nursing home and hospital, a home economics department, a public-health program and its training school, a surplus-food program and credit unions with twenty-three branches, island-wide.

Mother Mary Alphonsa, O.P.

The requirements needed for admission are simple . . . a doctor's certificate testifying to terminal cancer and inability to afford proper care . . .

THROUGH SPORADIC SHAFTS OF SUNLIGHT and pockets of deep shadow, Rose Hawthorne Lathrop, half in fear of the stares and unknown intentions of curious strangers, walked along down the tenement streets. This spirited daughter of Nathaniel Hawthorne had given up the social and literary circles of New York to devote her life to the care of the sick poor; had come from fashionable Uptown brownstones to the crowded slums of the East Side. She climbed well-worn wooden steps into the gray and cheerless building at the foot of Scammel Street.

In answer to the few who had dared approach her directly, Rose let it be known that she was there to offer her nursing help to anyone who needed it—that she had just completed her three-month training at the New York Cancer Hospital. A few hours later, when she went to the neighborhood grocery to buy a "necessity list," word had already spread around, and she was led by a grateful father to the bedside of his seven-year-old son. The "grapevine" operated once more, and in the next few days she was summoned on endless house calls, into poverty she had never known existed. And frightened people of all ages came to her door—to her "Relief" room—to see the "Lady."

Just a few weeks after she had arrived, Rose Lathrop brought into her rooms the first resident patient, a Mrs. Watson, who had been one of her first cases of facial cancer during hospital training. When she was pronounced incurable, Mrs. Watson had been dismissed from the hospital, as were all terminal patients, to face a helpless and hopeless future alone. Now she had found a friend.

A scant five months later, houses on Scammel Street had to be leveled

to make room for a schoolhouse, and Rose rented four rooms in Water Street, just a few blocks away. This sagging clapboard house, which received only the pale east sunlight through its paned, shutter-framed windows, was to be her home for the next two formative years.

Now there were three patients living in her hospital-home. Soon four more rooms were rented, and the roll of patients climbed to seven. The needs of her resident patients and the house calls to so many others began to tax the strength of Rose Lathrop, and she prayed that someone would feel inspired to join her; financial help from friends had kept alive her cause, but soon it would need more than that.

Then Alice Huber entered her life. A successful and well-known painter, she had long been anxious to go into some kind of charitable work, and a magazine article by Rose Lathrop had led her to an interview on Water Street. Now she stood in the shadow of the tenement building, wondering if this could possibly be the right place. Alice hesitated a minute longer, then stepped into the house—and found a cheerful woman in her late forties bandaging an old woman's leg.

Later, seated on the only real piece of furniture, a large green sofa, Alice explained her limitations to Mrs. Lathrop and admitted that she knew little or nothing about sick care but she felt a desire to do some charity work. These limitations were brushed aside and she began to come one afternoon every week to help.

Very soon she was at Rose Lathrop's side two days a week, and then

117

she gave up her own room in Brooklyn and came to live at the Water Street tenement. It was then that Alice fully realized the sacrifice and hardship of that life—an endless line of patients, work night and day. The women sat on wooden boxes and ate in what amounted to a communal kitchen, free for patients to move about. They were constantly surrounded by illness. The ceiling of their shared room leaked badly, and Alice knew soon enough the exact spots to place pans to catch the rain.

Helpful friends realized that their most urgent need was to find habitable quarters which would serve as a proper hospital and home. On May 1, 1899, the Servants of Relief for Incurable Cancer, as they were now called, moved into a comfortable old-fashioned house at 426 Cherry Street, where twelve and sometimes fifteen patients could be accommodated.

Shortly afterward, encouraged by a Dominican priest, Father Thuente, they became Dominican Tertiaries; Rose Lathrop took the name of Sister Mary Alphonsa, and Alice Huber, Sister Mary Rose. Within a year Archbishop Corrigan gave them permission to wear the full Dominican habit; and immediately after, they pronounced their vows. When someone suggested to

the Archbishop that it was a most extraordinary privilege to give the habit to secular Tertiaries, he answered, "It *is* extraordinary, but remember they are doing a most extraordinary, heroic work."

The new Sisters worked long and hard, and both their labor and their prayers were fruitful. New postulants came, and in 1901 a Motherhouse and novitiate of the congregation were established in a large yellow frame building on beautiful Rosary Hill overlooking the wooded Westchester countryside.

Faith in God and man was Mother Alphonsa's dynamic motive and it became her followers', as well. For twenty-five years, until her death, she worked for the ill and poor in the Westchester home. Sister Mary Rose carried on her dreams, and today there are seven hospitals and homes in the eastern states, a fine tribute to the heroic woman who began her merciful work in those three rooms at Number One Scammel Street.

Sister Dulce, S.M.I.C.

THE ALAGADOS—MUD HUTS WITH DIRT FLOORS, people barefoot and in rags, surviving on scraps of garbage . . . *Alagados*, the slums of Bahia, Brazil.

Drought-stricken northeast Brazil pours thousands of migrants each year into Bahia, and the end of the road for them is the *Alagados*. Few can find even the meanest of jobs; their position is desperate, they exist in conditions worse than those of animals . . .

Sister Dulce lay on her narrow bed, looking at the white guimpe and sky-blue scapular on the clothes hanger swinging against the dark-paneled convent door.

"Oh God, help me to help them . . ."

Help began when this determined, dedicated nun broke in a window of a condemned house, swept the floors, put down straw mats and propped open the doors to her first "clinic" for the needy of Bahia's slums.

Sister Dulce kept on breaking in windows and taking over vacant shacks as the need arose for more and more space for the sick and undernourished who came to her in droves. They were being sheltered in five of Sister's "clinics" when the Health Department served a notice, ordering her and her patients from the illegally occupied shacks.

Undaunted, Sister Dulce set up her clinic under some crude stone arches, the supports of a viaduct leading to the beautiful church of Senhor do Bonfin. She divided her shelter by walls of wooden crates, stacked by twos and threes to reach the stone "ceilings," some of which were only three or four feet high.

Only months later she was evicted again, for creating "a public eyesore next to a famous tourist attraction."

Forced to move from place to place, Sister Dulce at one time took over a deserted market; another time

she conducted her clinic in an alley next to her convent. But somehow she and her helpers managed to provide food, medicine and shelter through seven long years, when Sister Dulce's dream at last was fulfilled.

Her tremendous drive, persistence and belief produced a miracle; she finally succeeded in waking civil authorities to the urgency of her work. Help began coming in from all sides, and the tiny nun was able to bring about the construction of a hospital in the *Alagados*. Early in 1960 a hundred-and-fifty-bed hospital, the Albergue Santo Antonio, opened its doors to receive any *Alagadoro* who needs care.

Sister Rosalia, O.P.

THERE HAD TO BE SOME PRETEXT, any pretext—some reason, any reason—for arrest, even in Communist China that year of 1949. Christian doctrine and Communist doctrine had clashed head on. Sister Rosalia was arrested for possessing an ancient non-working table radio, on which she was accused of contacting Washington as a spy. To compound this absurdity, a small white packet of opium was planted, by the Peiping investigator, under a wooden water bucket in her room.

"It's opium, foreign woman," he said. "It's contraband opium. You are an opium smuggler!"

With that, Sister Rosalia became the criminal "Kon Niong (Unmarried Woman)," and entered the questioning room of Wee Chao's prison for the first time. It was a small room, ringed with dusty file cases. A bare electric bulb, dimmed and brightened by the uneven flow of electricity, lit a desk, a swivel chair, a straight chair for the prisoner and a cement floor littered with metal, leather, rope and bits of iron.

The questioning began. Day after day she was interrogated, and day by day she was told of the horrors which awaited her if she did not confess. She learned that the contraptions of metal and leather were torture pieces; time and time again she was threatened.

She was tied and gagged, hit with revolver butts, all the while suffering insults from her unrelenting questioner. "Sign this confession, opium smuggler!" In a small dark room next door, they tied electric wires, attached to a machine, around her legs and feet. It was devilishly planned to unnerve her, to break her will—Sister Rosalia was left alone in absolute darkness, waiting endless minutes in terror for the burning pain which never came.

After these sessions, Sister Rosalia was returned to a small room in which were imprisoned twenty-four other women. Some lay on the floor, each allotted a two-foot-wide space. Others slept on wooden bunks or shelves about four feet from the stone floor. Each night was a hell. Their cell was near the torture rooms and all night long, screams, curses and yells echoed down the corridors. The pitch-black of the long nights only magnified the terror of the agonized sounds.

Then came the picture-taking, and Sister Rosalia was seated behind a table on which lay the "evidence," the old radio and the packet of opium. A large number plate, 197051, was adjusted on her chest. Her veil was snatched off, the photographer ready for a tremendous laugh at the expense of Sister's embarrassment. But Maryknoll Sisters, as do virtually all American orders, wear their hair fairly long.

Twelve weeks after her arrest Sister Rosalia was moved into another cell—small, with a low ceiling of red tile, which, when heated by the August sun, created an oven. A four-inch shaft let in a small cylinder of dim light. In this twelve-by-seven-foot cubicle six women could just manage to make sleeping space on a brick platform which left only a foot-wide aisle at their feet. A simple hole in the wall was the toilet.

All night guards stalked up and down the damp stone corridors, stopping at every cell door to turn their flashlights on each face in turn. Prisoners dragging thirteen-pound ankle chains hobbled toward the torture rooms. Many of them confessed to nonexistent crimes to receive merciful escape by the firing squad.

Endless questionings filled the night hours. By day they listened to lessons in Communism. Wormy and half-cooked vegetables were their main food. A skin infection covered Sister Rosalia from head to foot. From lack of exercise her leg veins were distended and the numbness in her legs spread down from her hips. It became increasingly difficult to walk to the questioning room.

Then in October, Sister Rosalia was divested of her religious habit. The guard took her through the darkness, through corridors and across courtyards to an unfamiliar questioning room. But the same chief inspector was there, the same questions were there, the same tying, the same gagging. But even after four hours, she would not give the signal that she was ready to confess. In exasperation and frustration the inspector shouted, "You are a wolf in

sheep's clothing. Take off that disguise!'' With that he pulled off her veil and threw it on the floor. Soldiers removed her cape and long tunic and she was led back to the cold stone cell in her underslip. Substitute clothing, the regular Chinese woman's clothes of trousers and the coatlike *saam,* came from her cellmates.

Months dragged on. One by one the women in her cell had been called, and had not returned; a new purge was on and their places were filled quickly. A hundred and fifty new prisoners were brought in and the prisoners and cells were reshuffled in a night of terror. Just before dawn the guard shouted in the cell door, "Number 197051!''

"My execution day!'' thought Sister Rosalia.

But the door did not open.

About ten that same morning the guard approached the cell and once more called harshly, "Number 197051!'' But again nothing happened.

Sister Rosalia broke. In the dreadful uncertainty of that long day, she cried out in agony. At night she was called again; this time she was motioned out, and steady once more, the indomitable nun began her last walk to death.

The walk ended in the examining room again. On the desk was a paper, a "confession," which said: "I kept opium in my room and bought and sold it. I possessed an unregistered radio.''

Sister Rosalia sighed and shook her head. She would not sign—now or ever. They could use this signed confession to prove to the Chinese Catholics that Sisters were criminals . . . that Sisters dealt in the opium trade.

For the first time her questioner and soldier guards walked out, leaving her alone and untied; and for the first time Sister Rosalia had hope. Actually, the Communists needed to clear the prison. They were also afraid to execute her for fear that she would become a martyr in the eyes of local Catholics. They were not out to kill priests and nuns, their main objective was to discredit them. A few thousand foreign missionaries in China were not such a problem; it was the four million Chinese Catholics who could make trouble for the Party.

A shout aroused the Sister from her thoughts.

"Back to your cell!'' And they took her out.

The next dawn, "Number 197051!'' echoed through the corridor and the Sister's cell. Again, in trousers and *saam,* she was led to the questioning room, with the same guards and inspector.

"Here . . ." said the inspector, and he pointed to a heap on the desk in front of him. One of the guards threw over her arm the Maryknoll habit and remains of the veil. Her rosary came out of a file case and was thrown on the desk, her fountain pen and pencil, her mission crucifix, her medal—everything they had taken ten long months ago.

"Go to your cell and get your blanket and other baggage. The guards will then conduct you farther."

Sister Rosalia was released, carrying her bowl, chopsticks and quilt, but only after another transfer and a forbidding five months in a Canton prison, did she finally cross, half-dead but free, into Hong Kong.

Mother Paula, D.S.P.

ST. PAUL WAS AN APOSTLE. These Daughters of St. Paul are the modern missionaries of the press. Terms familiar to printers and pressmen, such as points, picas, fonts, lockups, galleys, proofs, signatures and folios, which form a whole special segment of our vocabulary, are just as familiar to these Sisters. It all began in Italy in 1915 to answer the need for a strong Catholic press, and on a clear June morning seventeen years later, the first two American Daughters of St. Paul arrived in New York harbor. Sister Paula, first down the gangplank, was greeted with a dubious welcome from Father Borrano: "But you're not supposed to be here yet!"

They had practically no money and definitely no English, but somehow they managed. Father Borrano and the assistant pastor of St. Mary's Church found a home for them—a five-room apartment on the second floor of a little house on Glover Street in the Bronx. The furniture consisted of a couple of beds, some chairs, a table . . . and their suitcases.

There was little to eat, often they had just a bowl of soup and a piece of cheese, or bread, milk and an apple. The Sisters were warned several times by Father Borrano that they might have to return to Italy; the wait for approval to remain in America seemed an eternity.

But in spite of these uncertainties, they began distributing copies of the Bible and other religious literature from the supplies of various parishes in the city. Through New York's busy streets they walked each day, carrying their heavy black bags packed to the sturdy brass locks. Each night they bound the printed messages. They folded the sheets with a little hand-fed folder, sewed the signatures together on a simple machine, and trimmed them on an antiquated hand cutter. All of the covers were made by hand; but they did use a small and ancient gilding press to print the titles.

Approval to stay in America finally did come, and in the years that followed, the number of Sisters increased and Sister Paula was elected Superior of an established Foundation. On the shores of Lake Erie they found their Motherhouse, a beautiful estate on which was a large house, two cottages, a summer house, an old stable and a small garage.

The stable gradually filled with a printing press, a modern cutter, a folder, two sewing machines, a back-rounder, a linotype, type fonts, an automatic gilding press and large piles of signatures, covers and finished books which brimmed over into the garage.

Mechanics explained the working of the new, modern machinery to the first Sisters, and in turn these pupil Sisters taught others who entered after them. As this pioneer foundation grew and expanded, it became basic to their mission to have writers and illustrators within their own ranks.

Sisters with such inclinations and talents are prepared for these professions by years of study. In their printing rooms and binderies Sisters move piles of printed sheets, carry trays of type, study a machine which refuses to run, mix inks for the press; proofread galleys, are busy at one of a hundred occupations in this modern mission founded to meet the challenging problems of a modern world.

Mother Paula, faced with a difficult transition from the security of the Motherhouse in her native land to the problems of a new country, truly succeeded in forming a flourishing, healthy community of Sisters who today are missionaries by way of the press, radio, cinema and television.

Sister Aquinas, S.S.C.

SISTER AQUINAS STAYED IN THE SURGERY long after Dr. Chao had gone. She walked toward the small laboratory, just off the operating room, thinking of taking another slide of the new spinal case.

She pushed the glass plate under the microscope, and sat with one eye glued to the eyepiece. Her fingers played surely with the delicate adjusting screws and illuminating mirror. At the end of the steel drawtube, in the brilliant radiance of the microscopic world, was the rod-shaped, acid-fast *bacille de Koch* that causes tuberculosis.

Ruttonje Sanatorium is different from other hospitals staffed by the Sisters, as it does not belong to the order; it is operated by the Hong Kong Anti-TB Association. Twenty Sisters, fifteen Irish, two American, one Australian and two Chinese, all Columbans, are here.

These Sisters, who in 1949 had been forced to flee their missions in China, had a language advantage as well as British nursing qualifications, and the Bishop of Hong Kong netted them quickly to staff the newly equipped tuberculosis hospital.

Tuberculosis—which thrives in the frightening living conditions of Hong Kong; since '49 over a million refugees have fled out of China into the tiny colony, creating unbelievable conditions of overcrowding, squalor and starvation. These elements provide the Columban Sisters with the challenge of facing sixty thousand TB patients in Hong Kong with only eighteen hundred beds in the sanatorium. Consequently, only patients needing surgical treatment can be admitted.

One of the two Sister-Doctors, Sister Aquinas, who received her degree at Dublin University, is a vital part of the team which fights TB by surgery. The sanatorium surgical team has developed a new method of surgery in cases of TB of the spine. This technique, which will save countless lives throughout the world, has already been used successfully on 300 patients.

128

Sister Aquinas pushed the microscope aside and
smiled. Her diagnosis coincided with the opinion
of Dr. Chao. The young eighteen-year-old with
the spinal TB would heal and live.
The slide had told her that it *was*
operable and her team could do it.

As doctors and nurses, the
Sisters take a deep professional pride
in their work. One of the Chinese Sisters,
Sister Thomas, said simply, "When I felt
I had a calling, I wanted to be sure that the
order I chose was efficient. Piety wasn't
enough. So I chose the Columban Sisters."

Sister St. Remi and Sister St. Damien, M.N.D.A.

THE REMOTE JUNGLE SETTLEMENT OF ST. CLOTHILDE squats on the banks of the Napu, a broad river pouring its waters south through dense Peruvian forests into the great Amazon. Here in St. Clothilde is a small convent, a school and a dispensary. From it Sister St. Remi, R.N., and Sister St. Damien take their knowledge, training and precious medicine to the Jagua Indians, who have lived on this river for hundreds of years.

One early morning the Sisters set out upriver in the "pirogue," a crude hollowed-out log canoe, with one Indian paddler. Tin emergency kits of water, food and medicine were firmly lodged in the unsteady pirogue, for what might be sixteen or twenty hours on the river and in native villages. Sister Remi and Sister Damien, who always work in a team, knew their first call. How many more calls they did not know, for by drums and just plain "river sounds" the Indians knew *they* were coming, with their gentle help and kindness. There could be many "unscheduled" stops.

The tropical whites of the two Sisters were unmistakably clear against the dark skin of the native paddler and the dense green and black of the jungle and the river. One hour, two hours, then three, and the pirogue was quickly tied up on the west side of the Napu, where an Indian woman was waving frantically. This was not their destination, but . . .

Sister Remi leaped from the pirogue, followed by Sister Damien with their kits. The woman led them in from the river by a short trail to a small clearing, around which were three or four huts. In one a child was moaning softly. Sister stepped through the crude doorway and stifled a cry. Lying on a bit of mat thrown on the beaten-earth floor was a boy of about eight, badly burned. She recognized him as one of the many epileptic Jagua children. At the same instant of perception, Sister Remi saw what had happened. . . . The boy had suffered an epileptic seizure and had fallen into the constantly burning open-hearth fire in the middle of the hut.

130

The team of nurses worked skillfully and quickly; the mother and father stood quietly, pressed against the far side of the hut. When the boy was bandaged and quiet, the Sisters went out into the bright sun of the clearing, and patiently explained to the parents that the fire should be built at a higher level to prevent such accidents . . . that another time could be fatal. They smiled gratefully and nodded. Sister Remi sighed and muttered to her companion, "I wonder, I wonder."

Another hour on the river and they reached another small village, where they had been called to attend a birth, one they had expected to be a difficult one. Two hours later, a Caesarean, another successful delivery—this little one would not suffer epilepsy as a result of head damage from the crude deliveries of midwives using methods hundreds of years old.

At the village clearing, two more patients were waiting for the "White Angels." A girl of ten or twelve with a swollen jaw and a man of thirty-five with a headache.

Sister Damien looked into the mouth of the little girl, who was holding a hunk of sugar-cane stalk in her left hand. It had to be another extraction—the girl had only five teeth left in her lower jaw; there was no way to save her teeth. Preventive measures had to begin with the babies and the very young with the right food, proper diet and precious milk, to replace the destructive sweet cane stalk which alleviated the constant hunger but ruined their teeth.

Sister Remi asked the man, "How long have you had this headache?"

"Oh, maybe seven, eight years!"

She had heard these same words before, from others, and could do nothing to help. These Indians pack anything and everything they want to carry into large net bags which they strap to their heads. These loads of as much as a hundred pounds are carried over rough mountain terrain for hours at a time, for the greater part of a day. The spinal discs of the neck are badly crushed or forced out of line and produce a "headache" that may last the rest of their lives.

Wearily the Sisters climbed back into the pirogue and returned, after a four hour trip back down the Napu, to St. Clothilde, to get ready for another day, for the hundreds of days and hundreds of people waiting for them.

That day had seen one young boy saved and a safety lesson taught; a healthy baby born, one day to be baptized and brought up with a better diet and chance to live; a young girl for whom there could not be much help; a man who was a prisoner of his cruel environment.

Other days would see better results, others completely discouraging ones, but these Sisters quietly continue their work with compassion and in hope.

Mother Mary Benedict, S.C.M.M.

ARRIVING IN MYMENSINGH, EAST PAKISTAN, just as that country was attaining independence, thirty-year-old nun-surgeon Sister Mary Benedict walked into a two-room shack. There was no electricity, no water supply, no medical equipment. This was to be her hospital, her sole companion a nursing Sister, and she was to be the only surgeon for six million people.

Even more dismaying than these physical problems was the suspicion and fear of the villagers of Mymensingh. For centuries they had been victims of suffering and disease, victims of the few "doctors" who had exploited them. A hospital was a place to die . . .

But this was a *doctor* and she needed a hospital, a dispensary, a laboratory. A well was dug; a power line was run into the native-brick shed with the woven-bamboo ceilings; an old U.S. Army searchlight was rigged for an operating-room light. She turned one of the two rooms into a twenty-bed hospital ward. Then Sister Benedict could begin her war on tuberculosis, tropical fevers, malnutrition, eye and venereal diseases.

The few villagers who finally came, mistrusting, were the most hopeless cases. But she couldn't fail . . . and she didn't. The steady, sure-handed, tough little Sister worked under these adverse conditions, winning the fight against accident and disease. During the summer, during the monsoon season, she often operated in temperatures above 110°, with the humidity close to the same sultry figure. In five years she performed thousands of operations, a third of them major. And in spite of the elementary equipment, the mortality rate was an incredibly low two percent.

This was made even more incredible by the cases which she faced; a man with an infected shinbone would most probably also have complaints of anemia, fever or hookworm. There was not one single uncomplicated case in the ten years that Sister Benedict was in the East.

The villagers who had been the most outspoken against the hospital and Sister Benedict came to love her as they saw the sincerity and competence, the success of the nun-surgeon. From as far away as two hundred miles the sick and the desperate made their way to her.

Now that the barriers of fear had been broken down, the need for a large and modern hospital was there. In Dacca, the capital of East Pakistan, four years later, a beautiful 168-bed hospital attested to the skill and drive of Sister Benedict.

Today, as the head of the American Province of the order, Mother Benedict travels thousands of miles in the United States, South America, West Africa, Uganda, Vietnam, India and Ghana, and returns to Pakistan about twice a year. Under her supervision are almost five hundred Sisters; doctors, nurses, laboratory technicians, x-ray specialists and pharmacists, all dedicated to bringing their talent and training to any who want it— Christian charity at work around the world.

Final
Profession

BY HER VOWS A SISTER IS DEDICATED TO GOD. In making her Final Profession, the Sister has given herself to the service of God and all mankind. The ceremony of the Final Vows resembles that of the Temporary Profession.

First, the Vow of Poverty. Enjoy everything, need nothing—in the renunciation of all worldly possessions she finds that she owns everything. She has everything to gain in this world and nothing to lose. It is another facet of the sublimation of self which every Sister strives to achieve and maintain.

This sublimation does not mean that there is a destruction of personality; far from it. It means that when self is forgotten, concentration on the job at hand can be total. The Sister is a member of the world family; her interest, released from self, ties her to the Sisters in her house, to everyone in the school, hospital, orphanage or mission in which she works. Her interest is as great in a refugee child on the other side of the world as in her own small sister or brother.

Second, the Vow of Chastity. Like the Vow of Poverty, this also widens the outlook and deepens understanding of love. Instead of a husband and five, six or even ten children, the Sister's interest and deep love go out to every child in her class, every parent of every child, everybody in the school, to every single soul in the parish, in ever-widening circles. There is not a single person who cannot rely on her love and constancy.

Third, the Vow of Obedience. A Sister instantly obeys her Superiors, but no one can take away her right to question the practicality of an order or demand. She can be sent to a small parish or a large one, to a hot climate or a cold one. But obedience must be reasonable and intelligent, and the Superior's authority must be legitimate before she can exercise it. There is always recourse to higher authority if one believes one's lower Superior to be unreasonable. A Sister's rights are always protected, she can appeal to her bishop or even to the Pope if she wants to. The ordinary living of obedience entails carrying out orders which she knows are intelligent and good and about which she has probably been consulted for her opinion. Superiors usually say, "What do you think about this, Sister?" before they decide on a course of action.

It would seem that religious life is withdrawal from the world. Sisters *do* withdraw from things worldly, but as these stories have shown, they are very much a part of the world and are all terribly human. Life under vows is not always easy; it is a constant struggle because these women are so human.

Values change radically for each individual from the time that the "freshman" postulant first knocks on the convent door to the hour in the chapel when the Sister makes her Final Profession. New values have replaced old ones; the spiritual serenity developed in those intervening years has stripped away any insincerity. The Sister is striving for real things.

The twenty-four hours of the Sisters' day is divided by the "horarium" of the convent, and most convent life begins at five in the morning. Usually they spend about three hours a day in prayer and with the help of the horarium they manage to cram more work into their day than most business people, housewives or general workers.

They are alert and aware, enthusiastic and industrious in their work; many a professional man has learned the surprising lesson from a Sister that she is not isolated behind those convent walls, and is quite ably prepared to do business with him in an informed way. They are capable, aggressive administrators of institutions, professionally aware nurses and teachers and productive writers.

A strong factor behind the hyperproductivity of most Sisters is refectory reading. The Rule of St. Augustine—the basic rule of many orders—says: "Listen without noise and contention to what is read to you at table, in order that not only may the mouth receive food, but that your ears also may be filled with the word of God."

This reading matter varies widely. It can be from books or magazines, newspaper editorials and speeches, political as well as academic. The daily ingestion of this sort of knowledge gives a well-rounded education to a Sister. For with her basic spiritual and professional training behind her on the day of Final Profession, she must keep up to date on subjects useful to her in her field —languages, medicine, nursing, teaching or social work. Wherever her work lies, a Sister who serenely performs at the peak of competence expresses best the spirit and purpose of her order.

Sisters living in convents all over the world have the same family spirit which knits them all together. Whether she is answering an emergency call in the giant hospital of a sprawling metropolis, or traveling jungle rivers in a wobbly dugout canoe, they are bound together by the rules of their order.

Sister Francis, cook, Sister Louise, doctor, Sister Victoria, teacher, Sister Pauline, secretary, Sister Suzanne, nurse, are not isolated strangers. They are truly Sisters together, working each in her own way, encouraging each other in their great service to mankind.

Acknowledgments

The following persons were particularly helpful to me in furnishing information and background material for this book:

Mother Mary Stella Maris, R.S.M.; Mother Mary Regina, R.S.M., Mother General; Sister Mary Stephanie Hanley, V.H.M., Superior; Sister Mary Alice, O.S.P.; Sister Mary Oliver, W.S., Mother Superior; Mother Mary Vitalia, S.S.N.D., Provincial Superior; Sister Mary Madeleva, C.S.C.; Mother Mary Genevieve, O.P.; Sister Cyril Edwin, O.P.; Sister Lucy, M.S.V.; Sister Joaquina Cjirbau, O.D.N.; Sister Mary Adolorata, O.S.M.; Sister Mary Lucy, O.S.M.; Mother Mary Romuald, O.S.F.; Sister Mary Sheila, O.S.F.; Sister Eleanor, S.C., Provincial Superior; Mother Mary Veneranda, S.M.I.C., Superior General; Sister Cristela MacKinnon, S. de M., Vocational Director; Sister Mary Joan, I.C.M.; Sister Mary James, I.C.M.; Sister Maria del Rey, O.P., Director of Public Relations; Sister Monica Mary, O.P.; Sister Eugenia, S.P., Historian & Archivist; Mother Rose Angela, S.P., Superior General; Sister Mary Augustine, S.M.S.M., Editor-Director of Public Relations; Sister Mary Grace, S.M.S.M., Secretary; Sister Mary Runelle, R.H.S.J.; Sister Mary Boniface, S.S.F.; Sister Mary Paula, D.S.P.; Sister Concetta, D.S.P.; Sister Mary Ransom, S.C.N.; Sister Mary Donatus, B.V.M., Director of Public Relations; Mother Mary Consolatrice, B.V.M., Superior General; Mother Jane Frances, G.N.S.H.; Mother Rita de la Croix, F.S.E., Provincial Superior; Sister Mary of the Divine Infant, R.G.S., Provincial; Mother Mary Hildegarde, R.G.S., Provincial Superior; Sister St. Gerard Mafella, M.N.D.A.; Mother Mary Hilarion, O.Carm., Secretary; Sister Joseph Julie, S.N.D., Provincial Secretary; Sister Vincent de Paul, S.N.D.; Mother Mary Elizabeth, O.P.; Mother Mary Michael, O.S.C.; Reverend Mother Prioress, O.C.D.; Sister Mary Pierre, S.C.M.M.; Sister Regina Agnes, C.S.J.; Sister Emily Joseph, C.S.J.; Mother Patrick, D.W.; Sister Mary Rose, D.C., Provincial; Sister Catherine Sullivan, D.C., Director of Vocations; Sister Mary Mark, S.S.C., Director of Vocations; Reverend Mother Superior, R.S.; Miss Mary Louise Mortimer, Editor, C.P.A. Member; Mr. J. E. Pridday, Jr., *Catholic News;* Staff of the Bay Shore, N.Y. Library.

138

A Brief Glossary

Advent The season of preparation for the feast of Christmas, having four Sundays and beginning on the Sunday nearest November 30, the feast of St. Andrew the Apostle. Since the tenth century, the First Sunday of Advent has marked the beginning of the ecclesiastical year in the Western Church.

Apostolate Designates the general work or activity devoted to the service of souls and the spread of the faith.

Ave Maria Latin, meaning "Hail, Mary." The first two words of the "Hail, Mary," or Angelic Salutation.

Beatification Preliminary step toward canonization. After investigation of the life, writings and heroic practice of Christian virtue, and the certification of at least two miracles, the Pope decrees that he or she may be called Blessed and honored locally or in a limited way by public worship.

Blessed Beatified, see *Beatification*.

Breviary The little black book containing the daily offices and prayers of the Roman Catholic Church.

Canon Greek, meaning "rule."

Canon Law The body of Church law, consisting of rules, regulations and laws regarding faith, morals, discipline and the conduct of ecclesiastical affairs.

Canonical Year One year of the Novitiate, subject to certain restrictions; limited visitors, a study of the Constitutions of the order and a thorough grounding in the vows of religion.

Canonization After the certification of two additional miracles, the final sentence of the infallible authority of the Church declaring that a Blessed has been received into the Church and, prescribing public veneration, has become a Saint.

Cincture A belt or girdle.

Chastity The vow of chastity is an evangelical counsel and one of the three vows professed by religious.

Cloistered A secluded order which conducts its work inside the convent walls.

Common Life Sharing every duty and activity, each hour and every day, in the convent.

Community A religious congregation of Sisters, a Sisterhood, an order.

Congregation A religious community of Sisters, a Sisterhood, an order.

Constitutions The system of laws governing any religious community or Sisterhood.

Discalced Latin, meaning "without shoes." Applied to religious orders or congregations whose members go barefoot or wear sandals.

Divine Office The official daily prayer service, the elements of which are psalms, hymns, prayers, readings selected from Scripture, the lives of saints and the works of theological writers.

Eucharist Holy Communion; Lord's Supper. The consecrated bread and wine used in this.

Friar Term applied to members of mendicant (Latin, meaning "beggar") orders to distinguish them from cloistered monks.

Genuflection Bending of the knee, a natural sign of adoration or reverence frequently used in the Church.

Gregorian Chant The ritual plain song introduced by Pope Gregory I and used in the Roman Catholic Church; it is unharmonized, unaccompanied, and without meter.

Habit The distinguishing dress worn by nuns. This nearly always is the common dress at the time of the foundation of the order.

IHS In Greek, the first three letters of the name of Jesus.

Incense A substance which, when burnt, emits an aromatic smoke, symbolizing the zeal with which the faithful should be consumed; also symbolizes the ascent of prayer to God.

Little Office An abbreviated form of the Divine Office, shortened to emphasize the quality of its recitation and to permit more free time to clergy and religious alike for their demanding tasks.

Missal The book which contains the prayers and ceremonial directions for the celebration of Mass.

Novena Nine days of special public or private devotions.

Novice One who, having entered a religious community, undergoes a period of probation in preparation for the profession of vows in the religious life. The usual period of novitiate is at least one year and a day.

Obedience Submission to one in authority. Higher obedience, or submission to lawfully chosen and approved superiors, is the principal vow of nuns.

Oblate Dedicated to religious or monastic life.

Office The daily service of the Roman Catholic Breviary. Also called the Divine Office.

Orders, Religious Although not technically correct, the usage commonly means any religious community.

Papal Decree Universal decrees bind all the faithful; other decrees bind only those to whom they are addressed.

Postulant A candidate for membership in a religious community.

Poverty One of the three religious vows, renouncing the rights of ownership and disposal of goods.

Province A geographical division of a religious order under the jurisdiction of a provincial superior.

Religious A nun, monk or friar.

Retreat A few days' withdrawal from worldly affairs for solitude, self-examination, prayer and amendment of life.

Ritual A book of prayers and ceremonies used in the administration of the Sacraments and in such functions as churchings, burials and blessings.

Rosary A string of beads used to keep count in saying prayers. It contains sets, five or fifteen, of ten small beads and one large bead. Each set (decade) is associated with a mystery of the faith or happening in the life of Jesus and the Virgin Mary.

Rule A complete set or code of regulations in a religious order.

Sacrament Any of seven rites ordained by Jesus; baptism, Confirmation, the Eucharist, penance, holy orders, matrimony and extreme unction. Also meaning the consecrated bread and wine used in the Eucharist. It is often used with the adjectives holy or blessed.

Sacristy A room in a church where the sacred vessels and vestments are kept.

Saint In the Roman Catholic Church, a person officially recognized as having lived an exceptionally holy life, and thus as being in heaven and capable of interceding for sinners: a canonized person.

Scapular A part of the nun's habit, nearly the width of the shoulders, worn over the tunic and reaching almost to the feet in front and behind.

Tabernacle An ornamental container for the consecrated host (altar breads), usually placed in the middle of the altar.

Te Deum A hymn of praise and thanksgiving sung on solemn occasions, and recited in the Divine Office at the conclusion of matins on feast days.

Tonsure The term applied to the shaving of the head prescribed for some religious and clerics. This is not common in the United States.

Vocation The call to a particular state in life. These states are the priesthood, religious life, the married state, the single state.

Vow A promise made to God, binding oneself under pain of sin, to the fulfillment of the promise. Public vows are made before a superior who accepts the profession in the name of the Church. The vows of religious are poverty, chastity and obedience.

Wimple A covering of cloth material worn over the head and around the neck and chin; part of the habit of many nuns.

Ecclesiastical Abbreviations

B.V.M. Blessed Virgin Mary
C.S.C. Congregation of the Holy Cross
C.S.J. Pious Congregation of St. Joseph
D.C. Daughters of Charity of St. Vincent de Paul
D.S.P. Daughters of St. Paul
D.W. Daughters of Wisdom
F.S.E. Daughters of the Holy Ghost
G.N.S.H. Grey Nuns of the Sacred Heart
I.C.M. Missionary Sisters of the Immaculate Heart of Mary
M.N.D.A. Missionary Sisters of Our Lady of the Angels
M.S.V. Missionary Sisters of Verona
O.C.D. Order of Discalced Carmelites
O. Carm. Order of Calced Carmelites
O.D.N. Order of Notre Dame
O.P. Order of Preachers
O.S.C. Order of Sisters of Clare
O.S.F. Order of St. Francis
O.S.M. Order of Servants of Mary
O.S.P. Oblate Sisters of Providence
R.G.S. Sisters of Our Lady of Charity of the Good Shepherd
R.H.S.J. Religious Hospitalers of St. Joseph
R.S. Sacramentine Nuns
R.S.M. Religious Sisters of Mercy
S.C. Sisters of Charity
S.C.M.M. Society of Catholic Medical Missionaries
S.C.N. Sisters of Charity of Nazareth
S. de M. Sisters of Mary
S.M.I.C. Missionary Sisters of the Immaculate Conception of the Mother of God
S.M.S.M. Missionary Sisters of the Society of Mary
S.N.D. Sisters of\Notre Dame
S.P. Sisters of Providence
S.S.C. Sisters of St. Columban
S.S.F. Congregation of Sisters of the Holy Family
S.S.N.D. School Sisters of Notre Dame
V.H.M. Visitation Nuns
W.S. White Sisters